TIME
TO EAT

Nadiya Hussain
TIME TO EAT

Delicious meals for busy lives

Photography by Chris Terry

MICHAEL JOSEPH *an imprint of* PENGUIN BOOKS

DEDICATION:

To the time-poor amongst us.
We rush, we scramble and we get by.
In doing so, we live.
Rushed and frayed around the edges,
still we go on.
We smile. We frown. Unsteady yet firm.
'I have no time' we say in haste.

Don't we?

We have it, no matter how swift and
meaningless it feels.
We have it! We have time, it is ours!
However long or short, it is ours to take.

Let's rush, but sometimes let's just stop.
To Abdal, Musa, Dawud and Maryam.

MICHAEL JOSEPH

UK | USA | Canada | Ireland | Australia
India | New Zealand | South Africa

Michael Joseph is part of the Penguin
Random House group of companies
whose addresses can be found at
global.penguinrandomhouse.com.

First published in Great Britain by
Michael Joseph, 2019
005

Text copyright © Nadiya Hussain, 2019
Photography copyright © Chris Terry, 2019

By arrangement with the BBC
BBC Logo copyright © BBC, 1996
The BBC logo is a registered trade mark of
the British Broadcasting Corporation and
is used under license
Illustrative icons copyright © Jess Hart Design,
2019

The moral right of the author has been
asserted

Printed in Italy by Printer Trento S.r.L.
Colour reproduction by Altaimage London
A CIP catalogue record for this book is
available from the British Library

ISBN: 978-0-241-39659-9

www.greenpenguin.co.uk

Penguin Random House is committed to a
sustainable future for our business, our readers
and our planet. This book is made from Forest
Stewardship Council® certified paper.

CONTENTS

HOW TO USE THIS BOOK

This book is unique and special because it introduces you to my world, my way of cooking, which can become your world and your way of cooking. It will help you become a time-smart cook without even really realizing it. I'm so excited to share all this with you. There are recipes that show you how to batch cook and how to use – and really appreciate – the space in your freezer. You can spin leftovers into whole new meals and make beautiful food that can be put together in very little time.

I don't want to appear condescending, I really don't. Or look like I know what I'm doing. But I kind of do! Not because I'm an expert, but because I know what it's like to have just one head and one pair of hands. We are all human. Cluttered minds, to-do lists that never seem to get smaller, stuff to do and still only four limbs. We can only get to our destination as quickly as our legs can carry us. We can only prepare the family dinners that are needed with the two hands we have and whatever time is left at the end of that day. Yet life seems to treat us like we are octopuses, with eight limbs to juggle the laundry, the chores, wiping down surfaces, tying laces, shovelling in food, typing, swiping, clicking.

I haven't got it all figured out. I still don't know how to do the YMCA and knead bread at the same time. It's a work-in-progress, but I will do it! I'm not saying my way is the best way. But it's pretty good. This is the way I have been cooking for a decade and it really does work. All you need is a willingness to change how you cook a little, and to make a little freezer space. It's definitely not foolproof. It takes time and a little extra thinking, but ultimately when I cook like this, what happens is I get my cooking fill, I get to be creative and cook delicious food. I get to cook in advance. By spending just a little more time in the kitchen (and by little I mean not that much more), it means I'm cooking extra, freezing and saving for the week ahead. By the time I have done this for a few weeks, I find myself with a whole week free to do other things. Like have a bath, do some work knowing dinner is sorted, simply enjoy putting one foot in front of the other without worrying about the speed at which my feet are moving. Leaving me happy to be human and less envious of our eight-legged sea creature. I don't want to be the octopus, I want to cook him, eat him, freeze him and enjoy him again the following week without breaking a sweat, without thinking.

This book has over 100 delicious recipes for you to choose from. Some take a little less time and others take a little more time, but there'll be a reason for it – you'll be creating a second meal to keep in the freezer, or you'll be using a component of the meal you are making to spin into something completely different tomorrow that won't require any preparation. Some are perfect for when you have no time to spare and others for when you have plenty of time. The difference with these recipes is that you have options. You can use frozen onions or fresh. You can use fresh veg or canned. You can make one recipe now and know that you have dinner in the freezer ready for the weeks ahead. You can make more sauce than you need for that dessert now and make a hot chocolate later.

In my first few weeks of cooking like this, I found I was busy cooking one week, cooking more than I needed, stocking my freezer and giving myself a week free of cooking, but safe in the knowledge that my family were eating home-cooked food. But after a few months I found I had food stocked up for weeks, so much so that I had to stop cooking for a while just to empty the freezer out. After six months, I was ready for every situation. Cake to take to a party? I had one in the freezer! Late home one night? It didn't matter because dinner just needed to be taken out and heated from frozen. Unexpected guests? I always had something to whip up fast. Late night? There was always something in the back of the fridge for when we got the munchies. If you want to test the theory, turn up at mine and I will have something for you – but I won't be slaving or panicking over a hot hob and a noisy oven.

I HAVE A FEW RULES
I ALWAYS TELL MYSELF:

1

DON'T THROW
ANYTHING AWAY

As long as it's not poisonous,
you can probably do
something with it.

2

CANNED, FROZEN AND DRY
ARE NOT BAD WORDS

They save time and money.
They keep for a long time
and save on waste.

3

THE FREEZER IS MY FRIEND

I always have one drawer totally
empty, having just that little bit
of space means you have room
to think on your feet.

4

EVERY DISH IS TWO DISHES

I always make a little bit more than
I need in the hope of turning one
meal into two, without having to
cook it twice.

5

EVERYTHING IS
AN INGREDIENT

You can make something
out of anything.

6

THE MICROWAVE CAN SAVE

It saves time and saves on the
gas bill. It's quick and really
very handy.

Throughout this book you will find lots of recipes where there appears to be just one recipe, but secretly there are two. It could be a double-up recipe or a recipe where you make a little more than you need, so you can make an entirely different dish as well. Don't be afraid if a recipe indicates it serves six if there are only two of you needing dinner tonight – you will most likely be able to freeze the leftovers, saving you cooking time later in the week. You'll find a short 'Basics' section at the back of the book, too, which contains staple recipes you might like to make yourself, if you have time, though the main recipes will just as happily work with the shop-bought version.

I can't promise everything, but what I can give you are delicious recipes that everyone can enjoy. What I can promise is a little insight into the way my mind works. This way of cooking has allowed me to free up time, and I reckon if you give it a go it can do the same for you. By the time you have gone through this book you will have mastered the art of cooking, eating, feeding and doing it all over again, without actually doing it!

Key

Each recipe shows an 'active' time as well as a total time, where relevant, to show you where you can be saving even more time (for example, a 2-hour recipe that actually only requires 30 minutes of my time – before the oven does the rest of the work for me – means there's at least an hour to spend on other things).

You will also spot some ingredients listed in green. These are where there are components of the recipe that can be doubled up or halved, and spun into a completely different dish. Just follow the instructions on each recipe. As you go through the book, you'll see the following symbols to help you plan your cooking time:

 can be made ahead   recipe is freezable   double batch

USING YOUR FREEZER

My freezer is my absolute saviour when it comes to preparing meals for my family. It took me a few years to work it out, but now I would not be without it. It not only means I can have stacks of meals in there, all ready to go, but I'll often have ingredients stashed away in there too, which saves any last minute trips to the shop when I've already whacked the oven on and the hobs are going! So, when my husband asks me, 'What do you want for your birthday?' before I can respond, he always says, 'Don't say a freezer'! I would have another if I had the room, but I don't! So I make do with the one I have.

You'll see from many of the recipes in this book that I like to prepare a double batch so I can freeze half of it. I often do this at the weekend, when I have a little more time and I'm always SO grateful for it when we're halfway through our busy weeks, trying to balance everyone's timetables and it feels like there's just no time left in the day for preparing a meal. If I can save on preparation time, it makes life so much easier in the long run. Plus a full freezer is better for your energy bills – there is more cold air to circulate around a half-empty freezer, so keeping it nice and full is time AND energy efficient! And that is also pretty ace!

You might think from the number of dishes I freeze in this book that I have an industrial-sized freezer! I don't, but I have learnt along the way that it's all about how you organize it. I've included tips on how to do this in some recipes where there's an obvious hack (for example, I like to pour batter into a freezer-proof bag which I then lay flat on a baking tray and pop in the freezer so it freezes in a thin sheet – far easier to stack and store than clumpy Tupperware when you're short on space).

It sounds obvious, but always label whatever you're freezing with what it is and the date you made it. It might seem quicker to put things straight in the freezer rather than hunting around for a Sharpie, but it will make your life so much easier when you can see at a glance what you have in there. And although you always think you'll just remember what each dish is, I guarantee you will spend a considerable amount of time trying to work out what unlabelled frozen blocks of food are once a few weeks have gone by. Just don't do what I have done and try and write on an already frozen meal – moisture and ink don't like each other. Label first, fill second! I also always have a roll of wide masking tape in my kitchen drawers, for the Tupperware that I don't want permanent writing on. Stick it on, label and date it and get it in the freezer. Then when you're done with it, peel it off and it's as good as new, ready for your next meal.

INGREDIENTS I OFTEN PREP AND FREEZE

I don't want to give you a definitive list of things you can and can't freeze, as this isn't intended to be a freezer manual. So much of it is learning as you go along, but if you find something you can freeze and I don't know about it, please tell me! Share with me on Instagram: @nadiyajhussain. We are all learning every day and I want to always be a part of that. You will find freezing instructions within each recipe, where it is relevant. But there are a few things I have learnt that it's always handy to have a frozen stash of. It's always a huge relief when I want to make something but have a vital ingredient missing . . . then realize I have a bag of it in the freezer!

❄ GRATED CHEESE (4 months) I always have this in the freezer, just grate it straight into the ziplock bag it came in!

❄ CHOPPED ONIONS (8–10 months) Be sure to double-bag these. They are so handy to have when I'm rushed for time, but I don't want everything smelling of onions so I always double-bag.

❄ MOST FRUIT AND VEG (8–10 months) that might be going to waste in your fridge. (If I think I won't get round to using a broccoli, for example, I will cut it into florets and freeze in a freezer-proof bag.) Just not (raw) potatoes or salad.

❄ MILK (1 month) I don't often have milk in the freezer, but sometimes when we go away for the weekend, rather then frantically trying to use it all up I just pop it into the freezer and defrost in the fridge when I get back.

❄ BUTTER (12 months) Often when I need to freeze butter, I mix it with a clove of crushed garlic and then I have garlic butter on hand whenever I need it, be it on steak or just to rub on to naan, it's there. Even better on a jacket potato!

❉ BREADCRUMBS (3 months) My breadcrumbs usually consist of the fat ends of a loaf of bread that nobody wants to eat.

❉ EGG WHITES (12 months) Freeze these labelled so you know how many you have in each bag, and you have egg whites for meringues whenever you want (for every egg white, you will need 60g sugar, added slowly to whipping egg whites and baked at 100°C/fan 80°C for 1 ½ to 1 ¾ of an hour till they are crisp and dry).

❉ SPICE PASTES (3 months) Store in a ziplock bag or sealed in Tupperware.

❉ PESTO As above.

❉ HERBS (12 months) This is really handy when you've bought a whole packet but only need three sprigs for your recipe, and will save you having to buy a whole new packet the next time you need it! You can freeze these as they are in a ziplock bag or zap in the microwave for a few seconds till totally dry then crush in the palm of your hands and collect in a jam jar.

❉ BREAD (3 months) and bread dough.

❉ CHILLIES (8–10 months) Again because you might not use the whole bag that you've bought. These can be grated straight into dishes from frozen.

TIPS FOR FREEZING

❉ MANY DISHES CAN BE COOKED FROM FROZEN, and these are indicated in the recipes. Remember that raw meat should always be fully defrosted before cooking.

❉ ALWAYS ALLOW FOOD TO COOL COMPLETELY BEFORE COVERING AND FREEZING. Putting anything that is still hot into the freezer will increase the overall temperature of your freezer . . . which may jeopardise all the other beautiful things you've already frozen.

❉ REMEMBER TO KEEP THE FREEZER SHUT IF THERE'S A POWER CUT. Your food in there should be fine for twenty-four hours.

❋ MAKE SURE THINGS ARE WELL WRAPPED UP. I tend to use reusable silicone freezer bags, or I freeze things straight in the dish I'd like to cook it in (such as lasagne, etc. – just make sure it's suitable for the freezer). If using clingfilm or aluminium foil, make sure it's really well wrapped and ideally pop in a resealable bag or a Tupperware container. This will keep your food free from freezer burn (although if you do find these little brown spots on food it's not harmful).

❋ I TEND TO FREEZE THINGS IN THE PORTION SIZES I KNOW I WILL NEED, which is often for all 5 of us. Try to do the same to avoid waste, as you don't want to be defrosting more than you can use.

❋ FOR SMALL ITEMS, such as falafel, freeze on a baking tray and then pop in a freezer bag once frozen (this will stop them freezing into one big joined-up clump!). Or just freeze them in a clump and then slam it on the worktop to separate them – that's the fun way to do it!

❋ THE SAFEST WAY TO DEFROST FOOD IS FOR SEVERAL HOURS IN THE FRIDGE UNTIL FULLY THAWED. If you want to speed this process up slightly, you can place the freezer bag or container in a large bowl of cold/room temperature water.

❋ DON'T REFREEZE FOOD ONCE IT HAS THAWED unless it has been cooked thoroughly (e.g. if you defrost some mince to then make into a lasagne which you cook, you can then freeze that cooked lasagne).

❋ IF YOU HAVE LEFTOVERS, BUT NOT ENOUGH TO FEED THE WHOLE FAMILY, I would invest in some small ovenproof single portion containers and when you have enough for a solo meal, freeze it. When it's late at night and you don't fancy cooking, and all you want is that meal you had last week … you can have it.

❋ MY FREEZER HAS BEEN MY SAVIOUR IN SO MANY WAYS. I want to be that ethical person, I want to do it all, and that's not always possible, but every time I save something from ending up in the food bin or I reduce a tiny bit of waste, I feel better. Because really, I'm no superhero. All I want is to save money, save time and feed my family – and when I don't waste in and amongst all of that, I feel a million times better.

BREAKFAST

Who says you can't have cheesecake for breakfast? Wrap it in a croissant and I reckon it's totally acceptable. These are so simple to make, and with lots of that filling left over, there's enough to make breakfast for another day as well, so I've suggested you make some Creamy Raspberry Overnight Oats. If you prefer not to make those at the moment, simply halve the quantities of the ingredients in green to make your croissants.

RASPBERRY CHEESECAKE CROISSANTS

500g ricotta (or soft full-fat cream cheese)

4 tablespoons caster sugar (or vanilla sugar, if you have any)

2 teaspoons vanilla extract (optional)

300g fresh or frozen raspberries

2 tablespoons plain flour

1 medium egg

6 all-butter croissants

Preheat the oven to 200°C/fan 180°C and have a 12-hole muffin tray at the ready. I know we are only making 6, but they just need a bit of room – plus I don't know many people who own a 6-hole muffin tray, I have never had one. I can't see the sense in making 6 muffins when you can make 12, but in this instance, it is perfect.

Mix the ricotta in a bowl and whisk to loosen, then add the sugar and vanilla and mix really well. Add the raspberries and give them a stir, so that they don't break up too much, but bleed enough to give that lovely marbled effect.

If you are making the overnight oats as well, place half the mixture in a Tupperware container with a lid and set aside – see opposite for how to use this. Now add the flour and egg to the remaining mixture and mix really well.

Cut each croissant horizontally, the way you would cut them if you were going to butter and jam them but not all the way through. Open them up and fit them inside the cavities of your muffin tray – you are aiming for what looks like a croissant shell cup. You might need to press lightly, to open the cavity. Do this to all 6 croissants, then fill with the ricotta mixture.

Bake in the oven for 15 minutes. There should be a gentle wobble in the centre. These are delicious eaten straight away, but equally delicious chilled from the fridge if you have any left over. They will keep for 3 days in the fridge.

If you plan on freezing them, pop them into a freezer bag (if you have several, freeze them uncovered on a tray for 1 hour first. Then pop into a freezer bag).

SERVES: 6   ACTIVE TIME: 10 MINUTES   TOTAL TIME: 25 MINUTES

CREAMY RASPBERRY OVERNIGHT OATS

Having breakfast all ready for you in the morning is one of the greatest ways to save time. While the croissants are baking, add 150ml of whole milk to the mixture in the Tupperware. Add 150g of uncooked porridge oats and mix through. Pop the lid on and put it into the fridge. The oats will be ready to eat the next morning, or the morning after that. You will have breakfast ready as soon as you wake up.

I like to eat mine with an extra drizzle of honey to make them a little bit sweeter.

This is one of those spur-of-the-moment breakfasts, for when you are unprepared and there's not much in the freezer or fridge – though once you are done with these recipes, you will always have food in the freezer! But for those very occasional days, this is easy, delicious and pretty quick. It's a really good way of jazzing up the humble baked bean. I'm using naan as my base, but you can use what you like, or simply whatever you have at home.

HARISSA BEAN PIZZA

2 large naan breads
  (or pittas, or leftover bread)
2 x 400g tins of baked beans
4 teaspoons rose harissa
a handful of baby spinach/
  2 cubes frozen spinach
4 eggs
4 spring onions

Preheat the grill to medium high and have a baking tray at the ready. Place the naan breads on the tray. Open the tins of beans and get rid of any excess sauce off the top, then pour into a saucepan with the harissa and baby spinach, mix through and heat gently over a medium heat.

Spoon the beans over the surface of each naan, and use the back of your spoon to create 2 little dips for the eggs in each one. Don't be tempted to add too many beans. If you have any left over, just decant them into a Tupperware container and leave them in the fridge, ready to microwave for another meal.

Crack 2 eggs into each naan, then chop the spring onions and sprinkle all over the beans and eggs. Don't worry if the egg runs a little.

Put under the grill for 5 minutes – this will just set the whites and leave the yolk runny, which is the way I like it. My husband cannot bear to eat runny eggs, so I would grill his for a further 3 minutes or at least until the yolk is no longer runny.

Serve and devour straight away.

SERVES: 4   ACTIVE TIME: 10 MINUTES   TOTAL TIME: 15 MINUTES

We love American pancakes but sometimes feel limited as to how often we can have them. Pouring and flipping can take time, so I have taken everything we love about American flavours and Elvis and made this recipe for peanut butter and jelly (jam) pancakes, baked all in one and then cut into squares. You can serve them with an extra dollop of jam, some Greek yoghurt and fresh raspberries on the side, if you like.

PEANUT BUTTER AND JELLY TRAYBAKE

3 heaped tablespoons jam of your choice (I like a berry jam, because of the deep colour and tang, or I just use whatever I happen to have knocking about the house)

3 tablespoons crunchy/ smooth peanut butter (or make your own, see p. 246)

cooking oil spray

250g plain flour

1 teaspoon baking powder

½ teaspoon salt

3 tablespoons caster sugar

170ml whole milk

2 medium eggs

2 tablespoons vegetable oil

icing sugar, for dusting (if you can be bothered, always looks lovely, takes so little time too)

Start by putting the jam into a microwave-safe bowl and heating it in 10-second bursts, stirring each time until the mixture is simply liquid enough to swirl around – we're not trying to warm it up. Repeat this process with the peanut butter (make sure to avoid putting in too much oil from the jar as this will just make the pancakes greasy). Set both aside.

Preheat the oven to 180°C/fan 160°C. Spray a brownie tin (approx. 18cm x 23cm) with cooking oil.

Put the flour, baking powder, salt and sugar into a bowl and whisk together. Make a well in the centre and add the milk, along with the eggs and oil. Whisk together until you have a thick batter. If time is even shorter you can make the batter in advance and leave it in the fridge overnight.

Pour the batter into the prepared brownie tin and spread out evenly. Take dollops of the jam and spoon them in sporadically, then do the same for the peanut butter. With the end of a spoon, swirl the dollops together slightly to create a marbled effect.

Bake in the oven for 10-15 minutes. As soon as the surface of the pancake looks shiny and not wobbly anymore, they are ready. Remove from the oven and cut into squares. Dust with icing sugar and serve.

These are great on the go, but you can also freeze any leftover squares in clingfilm.

I quite like the green stuff. As a child, very occassionally, I'd remove the stone and fill it with sugar – but the texture wasn't palatable no matter how much sugar I covered it in. But my goodness, mixed with all sorts of other things, it can be transformed, so much so that even my children quite like it. Versatile enough for toast, a dip to go with nachos or tossed through hot cooked pasta. Just not with sugar!

AVOCADO PESTO

1 small handful of frozen spinach (75g if you want to be precise)

2 small ripe avocados

juice and zest of ½ a lemon

100ml olive oil

3 cloves of garlic

60g walnuts, roughly chopped

1 teaspoon salt

1 teaspoon chilli flakes

Put the frozen spinach into the microwave for a minute until it has defrosted. By hand, squeeze out any excess water, then drop the spinach into a blender. Add the avocado flesh, then straight away add the lemon juice and zest to stop any of the beautiful green avocado going brown.

Add the oil, garlic, walnuts, salt and chilli flakes and blitz until you have a smooth paste. You might need to add 1 or 2 tablespoons of water to help it blend.

You can leave the pesto in the jar for a week in the fridge. The recipe makes enough for a few meals, so you're already ahead. Freeze in a labelled ziplock bag for up to 3 months.

Turn the page for my favourite ways to serve it.

continued over page ➥

MAKES: 1 JAR   TOTAL TIME: 15 MINUTES

AVOCADO PESTO THREE WAYS

My favourite ways to serve this delicious pesto:

WITH CHEESE ON TOAST

Lightly toast 4 slices of bread in the toaster. Spread a tablespoon or so of the avocado pesto on each slice – be as generous or sparing as you like, depending on how much you like the green stuff. Sprinkle over 120g of grated cheese and dab with Tabasco. Place under the grill for 5 minutes, until the cheese is bubbly and melting.

You could have this with a fried egg on the side or just eat it as it is (I quite like it exactly as it is).

WITH NACHOS

2 x 180g bags of salted tortilla chips + 1 x 300g jar of hot salsa + 180g grated Cheddar cheese + 1 x 215g jar of jalapeño chillies + 150ml soured cream + fresh coriander

Preheat the oven to 220°C/fan 200°C.

Spread the tortilla chips over a large baking tray. Dollop over 300g of hot salsa straight from the jar, then all of the avocado mixture. Sprinkle over the grated Cheddar and bake in the oven for 10 minutes, until the cheese is really melted and crisp.

Remove from the oven and dot over the drained jalapeños. Spoon over the soured cream and finish with a generous sprinkling of chopped coriander.

WITH PASTA

Cook 250g of pasta of your choice (penne, fusilli, etc.) according to the packet instructions. Drain, then stir in some of the avocado pesto.

I used to hate sticky rice as a kid, everything from the texture to the taste! But I grew up, revisited it and never looked back. Bitter gourd I will never revisit and will always hate. Sticky rice can be so versatile. Cooked with coconut milk, it's rich and creamy, and topped with tempered pineapple, it's even better. If you don't want a second batch in the freezer, simply halve the ingredients.

STICKY COCONUT RICE WITH TEMPERED PINEAPPLE

For the rice

600g Thai sticky rice

500ml cold water

2 x 400ml tins of coconut milk

1 teaspoon salt

For the pineapple

1 whole pineapple, chopped into chunks, or 2 x 432g tins of pineapple chunks, drained (about 520g drained weight)

2 tablespoons caster sugar

150g unsalted butter

1 teaspoon crushed caraway seeds

4 tablespoons coconut chips

To serve

cream

Put the rice into a medium-sized (preferably non-stick) pot. Add the water, coconut milk and salt, and stir.

Pop the pot on to a high heat, and be sure to keep stirring, otherwise the rice will settle on the base and will make that bottom layer stick. Keep moving the rice around. It will start bubbling and spitting furiously. Turn it down enough so you are not getting spat at. After about 6 minutes, it should resemble rice pudding – thick, with the grains clearly visible and very milky. Give it one last stir, then turn the heat right down. Pop the lid on and leave to steam for 10 minutes.

Put the pineapple into a heatproof bowl – if you are using tinned, be sure to drain off any excess liquid. Add the sugar and mix through.

Place a non-stick frying pan on the hob and add the butter. As soon as it is melted but not foaming, add the caraway seeds – they will sizzle. Add the coconut chips and stir until they are golden. Keep stirring gently, watching it carefully.

Now pour the contents of the pan over the pineapple and stir through.

Time to serve. We have made a double helping of the rice, so you don't have to cook it again, just reheat it. Leave to cool for another time.

To eat now, put some rice into a bowl and top with the pineapple. Apart from tasting delicious, your kitchen will smell amazing! Serve with some pouring cream.

The rice and the pineapple (if you have any left over) can be frozen in separate tubs. Or transform any leftover rice into a dessert – see Burnt Butterscotch Bananas on p. 223.

SERVES: 4, PLUS 4 LATER   ACTIVE TIME: 15 MINUTES   TOTAL TIME: 25 MINUTES

If I can cook and eat rice for breakfast, that in itself is a luxury for me. It means I have time for at least attempting to slow down. This is a mixture of black and white rice and so it has a gorgeous colour, topped with clotted cream and almond praline.

SLOW COOKER RICE

For the rice

cooking oil spray

100g basmati rice

100g black rice

50g butter

50g caster sugar

600ml double cream

600ml whole milk

1 teaspoon ground nutmeg

For the almond brittle

200g sliced almonds

100g butter

200g caster sugar

To serve

clotted cream or extra thick
  double cream

Spray the slow cooker dish with oil. Put in the two types of rice, the butter, sugar, cream, milk and nutmeg, then give it a good stir. If you want to cook it faster you can do it for 4 hours on high, but if you want it even slower you can cook it for 8 hours on low. I do this just before I go to bed so it's ready for when my kids wake at 5 a.m. on a Saturday!

Within the first half hour of cooking be sure to give it a stir, to remove any settled grains of rice.

To make the brittle, have a tray lined with baking paper ready. Put the almonds into a non-stick pan and toast them over a medium heat for about 5 minutes, until they are deep golden. Transfer them to a bowl. Wipe the inside of the pan and pop it back on the heat. Add the butter and sugar and cook, stirring, until the sugar has dissolved. Once it has, increase the heat and continue to boil for 5 minutes until the caramel is golden. Stir occasionally if there are dark spots.

Add the toasted almonds to the caramel and stir though, then pour the mixture on to the paper-lined tray, level it out, and leave to set and harden. When it has set, break off bits of it and crush in a pestle and mortar so that you have uneven chunks and sugary dust and all sorts. Pop into a jar ready for the morning and for plenty of mornings to come.

When the rice is ready, serve with a dollop of chilled cream and the brittle on top. This freezes really well in individual containers, making it perfect for an on-the-go breakfast that can be microwaved. You can also transform any leftovers into a dessert (see Burnt Butterscotch Bananas on p. 223).

We always knew when my mum was cooking cauliflower curry because that was the only way she cooked it. The gassy smell would hit us as we came through the door. Never enough to put me off the flowery goodness, though. Everything curried is delicious. But cauliflower doesn't have to be curried or permeate the air with its aroma – this is one of my fave ways to eat it. Hashed, with eggs.

CAULIFLOWER HASH AND EGGS

1 large cauliflower

1 large bunch of fresh chives

1 teaspoon garlic granules

1 teaspoon salt

½ teaspoon paprika

1 teaspoon cumin seeds

5 tablespoons chickpea flour

vegetable oil, for frying

4 medium eggs

chilli flakes, for sprinkling

Remove the outer leaves from the cauliflower and cut off the stem. Gently pull away as many florets as you can and, if you need to, deploy a knife to cut them away. You'll be left with the leaves and inner core stem. Set these aside – you can prep them for the freezer later.

Grate each floret into a bowl until you have done every single one. For ease you can use a food processor fitted with the coarse grating disc, but if you don't have one, the coarse side of a grater is ideal.

Finely chop half the chives and add them to the bowl, keeping the other half for drying. Add the garlic granules, salt, paprika and cumin seeds and mix.

Now add the chickpea flour and stir around to make sure everything is evenly covered. Because each cauliflower differs in size, and moisture, you may find that 5 tablespoons of chickpea flour isn't enough. Add a tablespoon more flour at a time until the cauliflower looks evenly coated.

Now add water gently in drizzles and mix after each addition. No exact measurement, but you probably need about a cupful. What you are looking for is a mixture that clumps together with no floury bits visible. When the mixture holds together and is not runny it is perfect.

SERVES: 4   ACTIVE TIME: 30 MINUTES   TOTAL TIME: 50 MINUTES

Drizzle a medium non-stick frying pan with oil so you have a thin, even coating on the base. Place on a medium heat, and as soon as the oil is hot add all the cauliflower mixture and flatten it over the base, working it up towards the sides a little too. Leave to cook for at least 6–8 minutes, or until you can see the edges becoming golden.

Use the back of a spoon to create 4 dips in the cauliflower hash. Now, one by one, crack the eggs into the dips, working your way round. I like to avoid the middle, as I serve it cut into triangles.

Pop the lid on and leave it on a low heat for about 10 minutes – this should give you a perfect runny egg, but if you like a firm yolk, leave it on the heat until it is the right runniness or non-runniness for you.

While that is happening, chop the cauliflower leaves and stalks finely, or place in a food processor, and put them into a freezer bag. I like to use these for making another hash in the exact same way as above, but using the bits that would otherwise go straight into the bin. They're also good for Spicy Scrap Soup (see p. 77).

Pop the leftover chives into the microwave and give them 10-second bursts until they are totally crisp, then crush them in the palms of your hands.

Serve the hash with a sprinkling of chilli flakes and the dried chives you just made. If you've made more than you need, you can put them into a Tupperware container and keep them for another occasion.

Yes, it's spicy food in the morning but don't be alarmed! Eating spices in the morning was entirely normal growing up, so when I learnt that it wasn't normal in every single home in the UK I don't know who was more horrified – if you like spicy food you shouldn't be restricted to meal times or rules. Give this a go – a little goes a long way, and it's wholesome and delicious and frankly a lot of fun. If you really want to balance things you could just have toast and marmalade for dinner!

MASALA PORRIDGE

For the porridge

150g porridge oats

1 carrot, grated

1 litre water

1 tablespoon ginger paste

½ teaspoon ground turmeric

1 teaspoon salt

For the tempering

100g unsalted butter

1 tablespoon garlic paste

1 teaspoon mustard seeds

To serve

Greek yoghurt

chopped coriander

sunflower seeds

chopped red chillies

Put the oats and grated carrot into a pan, then add the water and stir. Add the ginger paste, turmeric and salt and stir again. Cook on a medium heat for about 15 minutes, until the mixture is thick and bubbling away – if it starts to spit, lower the temperature and be sure to stir occasionally to stop it sticking.

A few minutes before the end of the porridge cooking time, put the butter into a small frying pan over a low heat, and allow to melt. Add the garlic paste, and when it is light brown add the mustard seeds. As soon as the seeds begin to pop, pour the whole lot straight into the porridge and stir through.

To serve, put a small ladleful into a bowl and add a dollop of yoghurt, some coriander, sunflower seeds and chopped fresh chilli, dry chilli or a grating of frozen chilli. If you happen to have any spicy seeds left over from the Thai Red Pepper Soup (p. 130), you could pop these on top for some extra crunch.

There is enough here to make several single servings that can be micro-waved, and this is a great dish to take to work with you, to eat at any time of the day. Store in individual freezer-safe Tupperware containers. Defrost in the fridge and microwave until piping hot.

SERVES: 6   ACTIVE TIME: 5 MINUTES   TOTAL TIME: 20 MINUTES

Every time I have moved to a new house, or had a baby, or needed to eat fast before an exam, microwave porridge has been my saviour, curbing hunger, satisfying and just getting the job done. But getting the job done can be delicious too. These are my recipes for microwave porridge in four of my favourite flavours. All you need is a kilo of porridge oats and a food processor. You can make all the flavours here, or simply make the one you want to and work your way through the rest, or better still, come up with your own.

READY BREAKFAST FLAVOURED PORRIDGE

1kg porridge oats, put through the processor enough to break down the oats but not to a fine powder

Apple and cinnamon

180g dried apples, cut with scissors into small pieces

2 teaspoons ground cinnamon

Bakewell

150g mixed dried berries and cherries

4 teaspoons almond extract

100g flaked almonds

Mango and coconut

100g dried mango, chopped

70g desiccated coconut

1 heaped teaspoon fennel seeds, crushed

Chocolate and hazelnut

50g unsweetened cocoa powder

100g chopped roasted hazelnuts

Distribute the oats between four 1 litre airtight jars, 250g in each.

To make the individual flavours, add the ingredients of your chosen variety to one of your jars of oats and shake around until evenly combined. Or mix in a bowl and then add to the jar.

To make the porridge, the method is the same for all the flavours. Put 6 tablespoons of the flavoured porridge oats into a large breakfast bowl and add 200ml of milk of your choice. Be sure to give it a good stir, then pop it into the microwave for 3 minutes.

Leave the porridge to stand for at least another 3 minutes before you eat it. You can sweeten it however you like – I like to add agave for sweetness – or you can leave it as it is.

SERVES: 8

ACTIVE TIME: 20 MINUTES PREPPING OATS IN ADVANCE; 5 MINUTES COOKING

Apple and cinnamon   Bakewell

Mango and coconut

Chocolate and hazelnut

As my husband always says, there is nothing wrong with cake for breakfast, and I could not agree more. This has fruit in the form of prunes, and granola, with a cake in between. All it needs is a good cup of coffee, or strong tea in my case, and that's not a bad way to start the day. Any leftover portions can be frozen.

PRUNEY GRANOLA BAKE

100ml buttermilk (but if you don't have buttermilk, which I don't most of the time, you can make your own by adding a teaspoon of lemon juice to 100ml of whole milk)

410g pitted prunes in juice, drained

125g butter, softened

200g caster sugar

200g plain flour

½ teaspoon baking powder

2 medium eggs

1 teaspoon vanilla extract

200g of your favourite granola (or make your own if you like – see p. 247)

If you are making your own buttermilk, do that now, to allow it time to thicken and do the science bit.

Preheat the oven to 180°C/fan 160°C. Grease and line the base of a 20cm x 25cm baking tin and be sure to grease the sides well too.

Roughly chop the prunes, then put them into the tin and spread them out evenly.

Put the butter, sugar, flour, baking powder, eggs, buttermilk and vanilla into a bowl and give everything a good whisk, using a hand-held mixer, until the mixture is super-smooth and shiny – this should only take about 2 minutes. Pour the mixture over the prunes and spread out evenly.

Top with your granola, pressing it gently down on to the batter so it sticks, and bake for 40–45 minutes. In the meantime you can get into your first caffeinated beverage.

When the cake is ready, a skewer inserted should come out clean. Leave it in the tin for 5 minutes, then either turn it out or cut it into squares in the tin and scoop it out.

MAKES: 16 SQUARES   ACTIVE TIME: 15 MINUTES   TOTAL TIME: 1 HOUR

My home-made Granola (see p. 247) is fantastic served with ice-cold milk or yogurt, but is also a delicious topping for the Pruney Granola Bake (see p. 43) or used as a layer in my Breakfast Trifle (see p. 47).

Trifle is not just a dessert, it can be eaten for breakfast too. This has all the layers and is as filling and as satisfying to the eye and stomach as a traditional trifle. I have increased the yoghurt layer here so that you can make some popsicles or other frozen treats. If you prefer to just make the trifle today, simply halve the quantities in green.

BREAKFAST TRIFLE

For the yoghurt layer

1kg Greek yoghurt

200g chia seeds

10 tablespoons honey

2 teaspoons ground cinnamon

For the fruit layer

500g frozen summer fruits

3 tablespoons icing sugar

1 orange, zest only (the rest of the orange can be sliced and frozen to use in hot and cold drinks)

For the bread/cake layer

175g brioche slices

175g of your favourite granola (or make your own if you like – see p. 247)

For the top

whippy cream, from a can

Start by making the chia seed yoghurt, so that it can begin to thicken. Put the yoghurt into a bowl and stir in the chia seeds, honey and cinnamon. If you have made the increased quantity, place half in one bowl and half in another bowl. Set aside.

Place the frozen fruit in a bowl. Add the icing sugar and orange zest and leave the fruit to defrost. Drain off the excess juice into a bowl for later. Place the defrosted fruit in the base of your trifle dish.

Rip the brioche into pieces and mix with the granola. Spread in a layer on top of the fruit and drizzle some of the reserved fruit juice over this layer.

Now spoon on the chia yoghurt (half, if you have made the double quantity) and leave the trifle to sit in the fridge for 30 minutes. Before serving, squirt on some whippy cream straight from the can.

CHIA AND YOGHURT POPSICLES

You can either transfer the remaining chia yoghurt into popsicle moulds and put into the freezer to set, or add the remaining juice from the defrosted fruit, if you have any left over, and some sliced strawberries and stir through.

Alternatively, you could pop this yoghurt into ice cube trays and freeze. Once frozen, transfer to a freezer bag. You now have a base for breakfast smoothies whenever you need them – pop a few cubes into a blender with some kale and pineapple juice, or a banana and berries.

SERVES: 6   ACTIVE TIME: 30 MINUTES   TOTAL TIME: 1 HOUR

I only started to make these after eating bought ones out of a packet, and while those are totally fine, this recipe is a really good way to use up leftover mash, but also delicious just to make when you have the time. Any leftovers will freeze well and can be toasted from frozen. I make them with turkey rashers and onions, but bacon or vegetarian rashers are just as good, and we like to eat them with roasted tomatoes and scrambled eggs.

TATTY CAKES

For the tatties

600g Maris Piper potatoes, peeled, boiled, mashed and cooled

2 tablespoons vegetable oil

6 bacon/turkey/vegetarian rashers, cut into strips, optional

1 clove of garlic, crushed

1 small onion, finely chopped

2 teaspoons salt

1 teaspoon black pepper

120g plain flour, plus extra for dusting

cooking oil spray

For the roasted tomato eggs

6 tablespoons oil

125g cherry tomatoes, halved

½ teaspoon salt

1 teaspoon sugar

1 tablespoon balsamic vinegar

6 eggs, beaten

a handful of fresh parsley/ chives, finely chopped

First make the tatties. Put the cooled mash into a bowl and set aside, then heat the oil in a small frying pan. Add the rashers and cook until golden.

Add the garlic, onion, salt and pepper and cook for a few minutes, until the onions are soft. Add the mixture to the potatoes and mix through. Now add the flour and mix until you have a stiff dough. Divide into 4 mounds.

Spray a good-sized non-stick frying pan generously with oil and place on a medium heat. Flour your work surface, then pat each mound of mixture lightly with the palm of your hand to form a rough circle about 1cm thick. Cut each circle into 4 triangles.

Cook each triangle for about 4 minutes on each side on a low to medium heat. When they are all done, wipe the pan ready to make the tomato eggs.

Add the oil to the pan and place on a high heat. Add the tomatoes (carefully, as they will splatter). Cook for a couple of minutes, then lower the heat and add the salt, sugar and balsamic. Cook the tomatoes until they start to soften.

Throw in the eggs and toss them about until they are cooked to your liking. Just before serving with the hot buttered tatties, stir in the parsley/chives.

SERVES: 4 (WITH SOME EXTRA TATTY CAKES FOR THE FREEZER)   TOTAL TIME: 30 MINUTES

Toad-in-the-hole is not just for dinner, it can be for breakfast too. This is simple and delicious, and everything is breakfast if there is brown sauce on the side. Sausages, mushrooms and batter … you can't go wrong. I've added some spices to this batter to give an extra punch – and the turmeric gives a lovely vibrancy to the dish.

SAUSAGE AND MUSHROOM TOAD-IN-THE-HOLE

4 tablespoons vegetable oil

12 standard-size sausages of your choice, pierced with a fork

400g mushrooms, halved

1 tablespoon coriander seeds, crushed lightly

For the batter

225g plain flour

½–1 tablespoon chipotle chilli flakes

1 tablespoon ground coriander

1 teaspoon ground turmeric

1 teaspoon salt

3 medium eggs

275ml whole milk

4 tablespoons crispy fried onions

Preheat the oven to 240°C/fan 220°C.

Put the oil into a 20cm x 30cm roasting dish. Add the pierced sausages along with the mushrooms, give the dish a jiggle to cover everything with oil, then cook in the oven for about 15 minutes.

To make the batter, put the flour, chipotle chilli flakes, ground coriander, turmeric and salt into a bowl and whisk to combine. Make a well in the centre and add the eggs and milk, whisking thoroughly to avoid lumps, then stir in the crispy fried onions. If you like, you can make the batter beforehand to save time. You can even make it the day before, but it will thicken overnight, so add a couple of tablespoons of milk and whisk up again if necessary before baking.

Take the sausages out of the oven and throw in the crushed coriander seeds – you should hear them sizzle and pop, as the oil will be very hot. Pour the batter around the sausages and put the dish back into the oven for 25–30 minutes.

Eat the toad hot, with brown sauce or ketchup. Add a fried egg if you like.

Any leftovers can be frozen, wrapped in parchment paper and foil, and can be reheated from frozen on a baking tray covered with foil.

SERVES: 6   ACTIVE TIME: 10 MINUTES   TOTAL TIME: 40 MINUTES

Frying has never scared me – it makes food taste delicious and creates an incredible texture that you can't achieve any other way. As if I didn't like bread enough, fry it and the love just strengthens. Dipping it into the sweet, fruity honey makes this one of my favourite breakfasts.

FRIED BREAD WITH RASPBERRY HONEY

For the bread

500g strong bread flour,
   plus extra for dusting

2 teaspoons salt

7g fast-action yeast

3 tablespoons vegetable oil

300ml water

oil, for frying

sea salt flakes, for sprinkling

For the raspberry honey

350g mild runny honey

150g fresh raspberries

To serve

a drizzle of honey

a handful of crushed
   pistachios (optional)

Put the flour and salt into a mixing bowl. On the other side of the bowl add the yeast and oil, then give it a mix and create a well in the centre. Pour the water into the well and gently bring all the ingredients together to form a dough.

Now knead the dough: if you are using a mixer with a dough hook, knead it on high for 5 minutes. If you are doing it by hand, knead it on a lightly floured work surface for 10 minutes. It should be stretchy and really shiny. Pop it back into the bowl, cover and leave in a warm place for an hour, or until the dough has doubled in size.

While the dough is proving, make the raspberry honey. Put the honey into a large bowl. Blitz the raspberries in a blender and then sieve to remove the seeds. Pour the raspberry liquid into the honey and mix. Set aside half the raspberry honey to use straight away and put the other half into a jar in the fridge where it will keep for up to a week. Perfect on toast or drizzled over pancakes or just on yoghurt.

When the dough has doubled in size, take it out of the bowl and knock it back, by giving it a little punch, then divide it into 16 equal balls. Have a tray at the ready, lined with kitchen paper, and roll out each piece of dough into circles to about 1cm thickness.

Pop a large non-stick frying pan on the hob and add oil to reach about 1cm up the side. We are only shallow-frying, so as the oil depletes you can just top it up. Heat the oil on a medium heat, then slide the first piece of dough in – the pieces should not touch, so fry just two or three at a time depending on the size of your pan. Fry for 2 minutes on each side.

When the bread is ready, take it out and sprinkle half with sea salt flakes while still hot. This half is for eating now – leave the other half to cool and freeze for another day.

To make this dish come to life, drizzle some of the raspberry honey over the bread and sprinkle with pistachios. Or eat it the way I do, which is to have a dollop of raspberry honey on the side, tear off bits of the bread and dip.

MAKES: 16   ACTIVE TIME: 1 HOUR   TOTAL TIME: 1 HOUR 30 MINUTES

When breakfast is presented as a crown you feel like you are living your best life. I love placing something right in the centre of the table before it is demolished – that brief moment of gasps gives me great pleasure. This looks great, and tastes delicious with the salty tapenade, strong blue cheese and a hint of rosemary. Not to mention the apricot glaze for sweetness. Any leftovers make a great snack throughout the day, or you can freeze them in slices for another time.

OLIVE AND ROSEMARY CROWN

250g strong bread flour, plus extra for dusting

1 teaspoon salt

7g fast-action yeast

2 tablespoons dried rosemary

50g unsalted butter

135ml warm milk

1 egg, beaten

For the filling

120g black olive tapenade

150g blue cheese, crumbled

To serve

3 tablespoons apricot jam, warmed

fresh rosemary leaves, thinly sliced

Put the flour, salt, yeast, dried rosemary and butter into a bowl, then rub the butter into the flour until it is like breadcrumbs.

Make a well in the centre. Add the milk and egg and use your hands to bring the dough together. Knead on a floured surface for 10 minutes, until stretchy and smooth, or if you are using a mixer, knead with a dough hook attached for 5 minutes. Put back into the bowl, cover with clingfilm, and leave until it has doubled in size (approx. 1½ hours).

Line a baking tray with baking paper. Flour your work surface and tip the dough out. Knock all the air out, then roll the dough into a rectangle about 33cm x 25cm. With the long edge facing you, spread the tapenade all over the dough and crumble over the blue cheese.

Roll the dough up like a Swiss roll, as tightly as you can, with the seam at the bottom. Take a knife and cut all the way across the centre, exposing the swirls and making sure you leave a couple of centimetres uncut to keep it attached at the very top. You should have what looks like an A that has not been crossed. Turn the cut side out so the layers are visible and simply twist the two pieces, one over the other. Pinch the end and then join the two ends to make a circle. Carefully place on the tray – if you lose the circle shape, now is the time to fix it – then cover with a greased clingfilm sheet and prove for another 30 minutes

Preheat the oven to 220°C/fan 200°C. When the crown has doubled in size again, uncover and bake for 25 minutes. When it is ready, place on a rack to cool.

Warm the jam in the microwave, just enough to loosen it, and brush all over the crown for a beautiful sweet sheen. Sprinkle with fresh rosemary.

You can freeze this loaf, or the leftovers. Cut into slices and pop into a freezer bag.

SERVES: 10

ACTIVE TIME: 30 MINUTES
TOTAL TIME: 3-4 HOURS DEPENDING ON PROVING TIME

This uses a simple brioche recipe, but it's stuffed with a banana and chocolate mixture and toasted in a waffle maker. What is great about these waffles is that you can freeze them when they are cool, without the toppings, and simply toast them from frozen in your toaster. Try different fillings if you like, too – frozen berries, jam, chocolate hazelnut spread . . .

BANOFFEE WAFFLES

For the waffles

250ml warm water

2 teaspoons dried yeast

3 tablespoons warm milk

2 tablespoons caster sugar

450g strong bread flour, plus extra for dusting

1 teaspoon salt

4 tablespoons butter

2 large eggs, beaten

cooking oil spray

For the filling

2 ripe bananas, mashed (peeled weight 200g)

100g dark chocolate, chips or finely chopped

1 teaspoon vanilla bean paste

1 tablespoon caster sugar

To serve

icing sugar, to dust

frozen yoghurt or ice cream

crumbled oat biscuits

toffee sauce, straight from the bottle

Put the water, yeast, milk and sugar into a bowl. It should start to froth, which means it's working. Leave it to one side for about 5 minutes.

Put the flour and salt into a second bowl and mix together. Add the butter and rub it in until it is like breadcrumbs. Make a well in the centre.

Add the beaten eggs to the yeast mixture, then pour into the centre of the dough. Using your hands, get in there and bring the dough together.

Lightly flour a work surface and knead the dough for about 10 minutes. It will be wet, and you may find you need some extra flour to bring it together. You may find it easier to do this in a tabletop mixer with a dough hook for 10 minutes on medium speed. Pop the dough back into the bowl, cover with a tea towel or clingfilm and leave for an hour or until the dough has doubled in size – this will depend on the warmth of your room.

Mix together the mashed banana, chocolate, vanilla and sugar to make the filling, then cover and place in the fridge.

Have a floured baking tray at the ready. When the dough has doubled in size, take it out of the bowl and knock it back on a floured surface. By which I mean get your fingers and knuckles in and squash it back down. Divide it into 12 balls. Take the filling out of the fridge. Flatten each bit of dough and lay them out on the surface.

Divide the filling between the 12 bits of dough, then take each one and pinch the dough into the centre to encase the filling. Pinch the edges hard to seal the dough, then pop them on to the baking tray seam-side down. Cover and leave for as long as it takes to prepare all your toppings.

Turn the waffle maker on and spray generously with oil. Pop a dough ball into the centre and push the iron down. Cook for 3–5 minutes, or until the waffle has a crisp golden exterior.

If eating straight away, dust with icing sugar and add your toppings.

Be generous, be frivalous and go high!

SERVES: 12   ACTIVE TIME: 45 MINUTES   TOTAL TIME: 1 HOUR 45 MINUTES

This bread is so easy to make and has all the delicious flavours of a spotted dick. Bread making can be fun and does not have to be laborious. Spotted dick can take a long time to make what with the steaming, but this way you can have those delicious flavours without spending all your time in the kitchen. This is a great time to make your own butter too, seeing as you will have all that time spare.

SPOTTED DICK BREAD WITH HOMEMADE BUTTER

For the bread

500g plain flour

1 teaspoon salt

2 tablespoons sugar

1 teaspoon bicarbonate of soda

50g vegetarian suet

100g candied peel

100g currants

1 orange, zest only (slice the rest and pop it into a freezer bag for extra flavour in cold drinks)

1 lemon, zest only (slice as above)

400ml buttermilk (if you have no buttermilk, you can make your own by adding 2 tablespoons of lemon juice to 400ml of whole milk)

For the butter

600ml double cream

1 tablespoon sea salt

If you're making your own buttermilk, now is the time to do it, to give it time to thicken and do its sciencey thing!

Preheat the oven to 220°C/fan 200°C and line a baking tray with baking paper.

Put the flour, salt, sugar, bicarb, suet, candied peel, currants and citrus zest into a bowl and mix really well. Make a little well in the centre and pour in your buttermilk, using a palette knife to bring the mixture together. Tip it out on to a work surface and gently bring the dough together, without kneading it – you don't want to overwork it. Place it on to the baking tray and flatten it down, then use a sharp knife to make 4 cuts all the way through, to create 8 triangles. Bake in the oven for 30 minutes.

While it's baking, make the butter. Put the cream into a mixer, or use a hand-held mixer, and whisk. It will quickly get to stiff peaks – just keep it going and then it will separate. This is exactly what you want. As soon as it does that it will change fast – you will be able to hear it. There will be a lot of sloshing, where the water separates from the fat. What you should be left with is crumbly-looking butter and liquid in the base of the bowl.

Have ready a colander lined with muslin, or a thin piece of cotton. Tip the butter into the colander and leave it for all that excess liquid to drain off. As the dripping slows down, give it a good squeeze to get rid of some more moisture. Add the salt and mix through, then set aside the amount you need for the bread and refrigerate the rest. It will keep in the fridge for a month.

When the bread comes out of the oven, leave it to cool on a rack for 15 minutes, if you can resist the urge not to eat it straight away. Then pull away the triangular wedges of warm bread and spread them with your fresh butter.

If you have any bread left over, slice it and freeze it. You can pop it straight into the toaster from frozen.

SERVES: 8   ACTIVE TIME: 30 MINUTES   TOTAL TIME: 1 HOUR

I think sliders are just burgers really, and as much as I like making them, I never seem to make the same version twice – when I really like one it always tastes different the next time round, so I always make these in 12s. That way we have the same thing each time and it all kind of happens in one pan. We love them for breakfast, but you can add a salad and turn them into lunch, or add fries and make them into dinner.

SAUSAGE AND EGG SLIDERS

oil, for frying

12 sausages

2 tablespoons onion granules

1 teaspoon garlic granules

12 eggs

1 tablespoon chipotle
   chilli flakes

salt and pepper

12 baps, batch baked so
   they're joined together (or
   2 x 6, whatever you can find)

butter, for spreading

12 slices of cheese (I like the
   stuff wrapped individually
   in cellophane)

sauce of your choice
   (I like brown sauce)

Preheat the oven to 220°C/fan 200°C, and make sure you have a roasting dish large enough to take all 12 baps comfortably or 2 trays that each fit 6. Grease the inside of the dish really well and line with baking paper.

Take the sausages out of their skins and place in a large bowl, then mix in the onion and garlic granules. Squash each bit of sausage meat into the roasting dish until you have covered the base, then bake in the oven for 10 minutes.

Meanwhile whisk the eggs well and season with the chipotle flakes, salt and pepper. Take the roasting dish out of the oven and lay the sausage meat on a baking tray. Grease the roasting dish again, really well. Pour in the eggs, making sure they reach all the corners. Bake for 5 minutes, then take the eggs out and place on top of the sausage meat on the baking tray.

Slice the baps in a clean sweep horizontally and take off the tops. Spread the bases with butter and pop them into the roasting dish. Lay the sausage meat and eggs on top, cut round each bap, then add the 12 slices of cheese. Squeeze over brown sauce or ketchup or both. Put the tops back on the baps and put back into the oven for just 5 minutes, to warm the bread and melt the cheese.

Freeze individual baps in clingfilm.

MAKES: 12   ACTIVE TIME: 20 MINUTES   TOTAL TIME: 40 MINUTES

Eggs are by far my favourite things to cook and eat. Not simply for their versatility but also for their ability to take on any flavour – we can make omelettes with them and bake cakes with them, and you can't get much more flexible than that. These rolls are lovely – the eggs glue themselves to the wrap so that they are easy as pie to roll, making them delicious and portable. They freeze really well, too, for a breakfast on the go and a makeshift lunchbox cooler all at the same time.

EGG ROLLS

6 medium eggs

1 tablespoon dried parsley

1 teaspoon garlic granules

½ teaspoon salt

½ teaspoon black pepper

oil, for frying

85g sliced black olives (drained weight from 185g jar)

100g fresh, frozen or tinned button mushrooms, sliced (optional)

6 small tortilla wraps

6 teaspoons sun-dried tomato paste

Crack the eggs into a bowl, then add the parsley, garlic granules, salt and pepper, and give everything a good mix.

Put a small non-stick frying pan (20cm or 23cm to be precise) on the hob on a medium heat, and drizzle in 2 teaspoons of oil.

Take the time at this stage to peel your tortilla wraps away from each other, otherwise you will be frustrated when you can't get them separated, and frustration leaves you with big holes in your tortillas.

Put the olives into a bowl, and the sliced mushrooms, if using, in another bowl, and have them nearby. Pour 3 tablespoons of the egg mixture into the pan – the eggs should sizzle, but if they don't, turn the heat up a little. Scatter a few olive slices and mushrooms on to the wet egg mix.

Take a tortilla wrap and spread it with a teaspoon of sun-dried tomato paste. Quickly put the tortilla on top of the egg, paste side down. While the wrap and egg are cooking, get the next wrap ready, spread with the paste.

Using the back of a slotted spatula, press the top of the tortilla to help distribute the egg under the wrap. Cook for no more than 30 seconds, then, as soon as the egg has glued itself to the tortilla, flip over and cook on the other side just to warm it through for another 30 seconds.

Take the pan off the heat and put the tortilla/egg on a plate. Roll the whole thing when it is cool enough to touch. Do the same with the rest of the wraps until the egg is used up.

Wrap any leftovers in clingfilm and pop them into the freezer.

When you are ready to eat the leftovers, leave to thaw in the fridge. Or microwave with clingfilm still on for 1 minute on high, until hot all the way through. Keep heating in 10 second bursts, if needed.

SERVES: 6   TOTAL TIME: 20 MINUTES

I love making this – the muffins are filled with tangy sun-dried tomato and cheese, covered with a cheesy sauce and grilled. It's warm and wonderful and there is a double helping of sauce to freeze for a macaroni cheese another time (see below in green or just halve the sauce ingredients, if you don't want to do this).

ENGLISH MUFFIN BAKE

7 English muffins

10 tablespoons sun-dried tomato paste

100g Cheddar cheese, grated

For the cheese sauce

60g butter

60g plain flour

1.2 litres whole milk

½ teaspoon salt

1 tablespoon yeast extract

100g Cheddar cheese, grated

Preheat the oven to 220°C/fan 200°C and have a 900g loaf tin at the ready.

Melt the butter in a pan, then add the flour and whisk into a smooth paste. Pour in the milk a little at a time, making sure to keep mixing – the mixture needs to come back to the boil before each milk addition. Cook on a low heat for 5 minutes, then take off the heat. Stir in the salt and yeast extract, then add the cheese and stir through.

Toast the muffins and slice them in half. Spread both cut sides with the sun-dried tomato paste and sprinkle with a little of the cheese, then sandwich them back together. Spread a little cheese sauce in the base of the loaf tin. Line the muffins up next to each other in the tin and pour half the remaining sauce all over them, making sure you get the sauce into all the gaps. Top with the rest of the cheese and bake for 30 minutes, until the top is really crisp.

MACARONI CHEESE

You can freeze the rest of the cheese sauce for another time, or make a macaroni cheese now so that you have a dinner to eat at some point in the next few days. Cook 250g of macaroni and drain, then add to the sauce and stir through. Pour into an ovenproof freezer-safe dish, and sprinkle with grated cheese. Leave to cool, then freeze until needed. To cook, preheat the oven to 200°C/fan 180°C and bake uncovered for 40 minutes.

SERVES: 4–6   ACTIVE TIME: 30 MINUTES   TOTAL TIME: 1 HOUR

These are like crumpets, but thinner and with no need for a special mould to make them. They are satisfying to make as you watch the bubbles come to the surface. These are made with cocoa, so they have a subtle chocolate flavour. Served with whipped butter – yes!

COCOA PIKELETS WITH WHIPPED MAPLE BUTTER

For the pikelets

500g strong bread flour

50g cocoa powder

7g fast-action yeast

2 teaspoons caster sugar

350ml warm water

350ml milk

cooking oil spray

For the whipped maple butter

150g butter, softened

8 teaspoons maple syrup

Begin by making the pikelets. Put the flour and cocoa powder into a bowl, then stir in the yeast and sugar. Now add the water and milk, and whisk to bring the whole thing together into a smooth paste. Cover and leave in a warm place until it has doubled in size and is bubbly.

While that happens, make the whipped butter. Put the butter into a small bowl along with 2 teaspoons of the maple syrup. Whip for 2 minutes on high, then pop into the freezer for 2 minutes.

Now take the butter out, add another 2 teaspoons of maple syrup, and whip for another 2 minutes. Then put back into the freezer for 2 minutes. Take it out again, add 2 more teaspoons of maple syrup and whip for a further 2 minutes. Then put back into the freezer, again, for 2 minutes.

Then for the last time, take it out, add another 2 teaspoons of maple syrup, whip and pop into a serving dish.

Once the dough has doubled in size, spray a non-stick frying pan with oil and place on a medium heat. Put 2 tablespoons of the dough mix into the pan to form each pikelet. They shouldn't touch while cooking, so you may have to do this in several batches to avoid crowding the pan. Cook gently for 2 minutes, or until the surface looks dry and matt. Then turn them over and cook for 30 seconds.

The pikelets are best eaten warm with lashings of the whipped butter, or cold later. Freeze between layers of parchment paper and pop into a freezer bag.

MAKES: 30   ACTIVE TIME: 30 MINUTES   TOTAL TIME: 1 HOUR 45 MINUTES

Scones are one of the first things most kids learn to bake, especially at secondary school. So varying them is a load of fun, and to have them for breakfast is even better. These ones are cheesy and spread with a delicious mustardy paste.

PARMESAN SCONES WITH SALMON PASTE

For the Parmesan scones

450g self-raising flour

110g butter, cubed

½ teaspoon baking powder

½ teaspoon salt

1 teaspoon onion granules

1 tablespoon dried chives

50g Parmesan cheese, plus
   a little extra for sprinkling

300ml whole milk

1 egg, for glazing

For the salmon paste

120g smoked salmon
   trimmings

1 tablespoon wholegrain
   mustard

½ teaspoon salt

a sprinkling of black pepper

5 tablespoons Greek
   yoghurt/crème fraîche

Preheat the oven to 220°C/fan 200°C. Lightly grease two baking sheets.

Put the flour and butter into a bowl and rub together with your fingertips until it is like breadcrumbs. Add the baking powder, salt, onion granules, chives and cheese and mix through really well. Make a well in the centre and pour in all the milk, then bring the dough together into one large mound.

Roll the dough out on a flour-dusted work surface to a thickness of 2cm, making sure to keep it to a rectangular shape. Using a sharp knife, cut it into 18 squares and place them on the baking trays a few centimetres apart. Brush with egg, sprinkle with Parmesan and bake for 12–15 minutes.

To make the salmon paste, put the salmon, mustard, salt, pepper and yoghurt into a blender and blitz.

When the scones are ready, put them on a rack to cool. Freeze half of them in bags and eat the other half spread with the salmon paste.

MAKES: 18   ACTIVE TIME: 30 MINUTES   TOTAL TIME: 45 MINUTES

This is like meatloaf meets Wellington meets sausage roll. Which can never really be a bad thing. With a line of hard-boiled eggs hidden inside, it's delicious for breakfast but also pretty delicious, cold sliced, between a soft, floury, heavily buttered bap. Makes a great snack throughout the day – and it's perfect for picnics.

MEATLOAF ROLL

500g lean beef mince

6 sausages, taken out of their skins

1 teaspoon chilli flakes

1 teaspoon salt

2 cloves of garlic, crushed

1 small onion, finely chopped

1 slice of bread, blitzed into breadcrumbs, or 5 tablespoons dried breadcrumbs

a large handful of fresh parsley

5 hard-boiled eggs (boiled for 8 minutes, then plunged into cold water), peeled

500g ready-rolled puff pastry

3 teaspoons yeast extract, mixed with 1 teaspoon warm water

1 egg, beaten, for eggwash

Preheat the oven to 200°C/fan 180°C.

Put the mince, sausage meat, chilli flakes, salt, garlic, onion and bread-crumbs into a bowl and mix together with your hands. Add the parsley and mix until you have flecks of green all through the meat mixture.

Lay two long lengths of clingfilm on your worktop, one overlapping the other. Turn the meat mixture on to it and pat it out with damp hands into a rectangular shape about 30cm x 25cm. Line up the hard-boiled eggs in a row down the centre of the rectangle, short end to short end. With the aid of the clingfilm, create a large sausage shape. The eggs should be encased by the meat, rather like a long Scotch egg. Twist the ends of the clingfilm and put the roll into the fridge.

Meanwhile, roll out the pastry to about 35cm x 35cm and 5mm thickness and brush the surface with the yeast extract mix. Remove the meat roll from the clingfilm and place lengthways on the rolled-out pastry, just off centre. Bring the larger side of the pastry over the meat roll, then pinch the edges together to close. Crimp all the way round.

Brush the pastry with the egg wash and place on a baking tray. Put it into the preheated oven and bake for about 1 hour, or until the pastry is golden and the roll is cooked through.

TO GET AHEAD

If you want to get ahead, you can prepare all this the night before and bake it in the morning. After brushing the roll with the eggwash, wrap it in clingfilm and place it in the fridge on its baking tray overnight. The following morning, preheat the oven to 200°C/fan 180°C, remove the clingfilm, and cook the roll for 45 minutes. Reduce the temperature to 180°C/fan 160°C and bake for a further 30 minutes, until cooked through.

SERVES: 8   ACTIVE TIME: 1 HOUR   TOTAL TIME: 2 HOURS

LUNCH

I love anything where as little cooking as possible is required – not because I don't like cooking, it's just that sometimes I don't want to do it. All you need for this is a blender, smoothie maker or processor – whatever you use to make mush – it will work, and the only cooking is the pasta. This tastes delicious but my goodness, the colour! This recipe will give you two portions of the glorious beetroot sauce; but if you just want to make a single batch today, halve the ingredients in green.

BLENDER BEETROOT

500g pasta

600g cooked beetroot, drained

100ml olive oil

1 teaspoon fine salt

4 cloves of garlic

1 large red chilli (deseeded if you don't want it too spicy)

200g feta cheese

20g fresh dill, finely chopped

1 tablespoon lemon juice, out of a bottle

extra olive oil, for serving

Cook the pasta as per the instructions on the packet.

Meanwhile make the sauce. Put the beetroot into a blender and add the olive oil, salt, garlic and chilli. Blend to a smooth paste.

Put half the sauce into a small ziplock freezer bag, seal and freeze. Now you have another batch of the sauce ready for another meal.

Crumble the feta cheese and place in a bowl. Chop the dill and add to the cheese, then drizzle over the lemon juice and mix.

Once the pasta is cooked to your liking (I like it a little bit firm), drain and put back into the pan. Pour in all that beautiful beetroot sauce and mix through. I can't help but be mesmerized by nature when the colour mixes with the pasta, staining it bright pink.

Tip it out on to a serving dish and sprinkle over all the feta and dill mix. Drizzle with a little extra oil for good measure before serving.

The frozen sauce will keep for up to 6 months. Store in a labelled ziplock bag.

SERVES: 5   TOTAL TIME: 10 MINUTES

I never ate these freezer aisle equivalents until I made a trip to a specialist freezer supermarket. I absolutely loved them! But as with most things, I dissected them and made my own version, with no less than three cheeses and a dip to go with them. We make 8 here, which will either serve 4 very hungry people, or you can pop a few in the freezer to have your own homemade version ready as instantly as the shop-bought variety!

THREE CHEESE CRISPY PANCAKES

For the crispy pancakes

250g mascarpone

25ml whole milk

150g any hard cheese
  (I like a combo of red
  Leicester, mature Cheddar
  and Parmesan)

2 cloves of garlic, crushed

1 medium red onion,
  chopped

8 crêpe pancakes

4 eggs, beaten

300g golden breadcrumbs

cooking oil spray

For the sauce

1 x 215g jar of jalapeños,
  drained

75ml olive oil

a pinch of salt

a small handful of fresh
  mint leaves

Mix the mascarpone with the milk and blend to a smooth paste. Stir in the cheese, garlic and chopped onion.

Have ready a baking tray that fits in the freezer. Lay out the pancakes on a work surface and divide the filling mixture between the centres. Brush the edges very lightly with the beaten egg, then fold them over and press together to create semicircles, firmly so they stick together. Flatten them a bit with your hand, then place on the tray and put them straight into the freezer. To save space you can freeze one layer of pancakes on top of the other, with sheets of baking paper in between.

Preheat the oven to 200°C/fan 180°C and have two greased baking trays ready. Have the whisked eggs ready on a plate with sides, and the breadcrumbs on another. Take the pancakes out of the freezer, dip them into the egg and then into the breadcrumbs, then pop them on to the trays. Press down and really push the crumbs into the egg so they stick. Spray the pancakes generously with oil and bake for 30 minutes, until crisp and golden.

To make the sauce, put the jalapeños, oil, salt and mint into a blender and whiz to a smooth sauce. I like to use the sauce as a drizzle over a simple leaf salad or just as a dip.

Once cooked, the pancakes can be frozen.

SERVES: 4 (WITH SOME
FOR LATER, IF YOU'RE
NOT TOO HUNGRY TODAY)   ACTIVE TIME: 30 MINUTES   TOTAL TIME: 1 HOUR

For a quick meal, quesadillas are my favourite thing to make when I have roast chicken left over from Sunday dinner. But I always have roasted chicken breasts in the freezer – you can buy them by the bagful – something that was my saving grace a few years ago when we were ferrying the kids between one after-school activity and the next. This is what I love to do with leftover or pre-cooked chicken, keeping it fresh with the flavours of tzatziki and adding cheese to melt the quesadillas together – they are firmly up there as a total fave in our house.

TZATZIKI QUESADILLAS

350g roasted chicken breast, sliced (or scraps off a roasted chicken carcass)

½ a cucumber, grated

2 tablespoons Greek yoghurt

1 teaspoon dried mint

1 teaspoon garlic granules

2 teaspoon za'atar (you can find this with the spices in the supermarket aisle)

½ teaspoon salt

120g Cheddar cheese, grated

1 x 215g jar of jalapeños, drained

5 large tortilla wraps

cooking oil spray

Put the chicken into a bowl. Squeeze any excess juice out of the grated cucumber and add to the bowl, then stir in the yoghurt, mint, garlic granules, za'atar, salt and cheese. Chop the jalapeños and stir through the chicken mix.

Spread the filling over one half of each tortilla, making sure to spread it all the way to the edge, then fold over. Do the same with the other 4 tortillas.

Pop a griddle pan on the heat and spray it with oil. Cook one tortilla at a time, using a slotted turner to press down so the cheese melts and helps to stick the wrap together. Cook for 3 minutes on each side.

If you are serving these at a get-together, leave them to cool slightly and cut them into smaller triangles, but otherwise just cut them in half and serve.

Leftovers freeze well, and can be heated from frozen.

The filling can be kept in the fridge for 5 days, and is great with a jacket potato if you don't fancy quesadillas again.

SERVES: 5   TOTAL TIME: 45 MINUTES

This lentil and orange combo is one of my favourites. Lentils were a staple when I was growing up and they still are. I love them, and so do my children, so I have found loads of ways of cooking them, some traditional and others a bit less traditional. They work brilliantly to thicken up a soup. And once a soup is made, you have one of the quickest lunches all ready to go in your fridge or freezer.

LENTIL AND ORANGE SOUP

300g split red lentils

2 litres cold water

1 teaspoon baking powder

2 teaspoons ground turmeric

1½–2 teaspoons salt

1–2 teaspoons chilli flakes

150ml vegetable oil

8 cloves of garlic, crushed

2 teaspoons coriander seeds, crushed

zest and juice of 2 large oranges

To serve

fresh coriander

cream, to drizzle

crusty bread

Put the lentils into a large saucepan, then wash and rinse them until the water runs clear. Drain, then put them back into the saucepan and add 2 litres of cold water.

Add the baking powder – this helps to retain a bold colour. Add the turmeric, salt and chilli flakes. Stir it, otherwise it will all just sit on the surface. Pop the pan on to a high heat and bring to the boil, stirring all the time. You have to stir to stop the lentils sticking in the first instance. As soon as it has boiled, leave it on a medium heat to simmer away.

After half an hour, put the oil into a small pan over a high heat, then add the garlic and cook till golden brown. Add the coriander seeds and as soon as they start to pop, pour the mixture into the lentils and stir through.

To finish, add the zest and juice of the oranges and simmer for another 5 minutes. Take off the heat and serve with chopped coriander, a drizzle of cream and some crusty bread.

If you have any soup left over you can let it cool, then put it into individual portions in Tupperware containers and freeze.

SERVES: 6–8   ACTIVE TIME: 15 MINUTES   TOTAL TIME: 40 MINUTES

I have been saving scraps for as long as I can remember. I started when I began weaning my second little boy. I needed to save money and we had to find ways to waste less, eat comfortably and not be totally short at the end of the month. It seemed mindless to throw away these beautiful peelings, the most nutritious and delicious part of most root veg, full of flavour and full of fibre, and it helped my conscience as well as my wallet. The scraps developed from baby foods to peelings I would deep-fry to soup. This recipe varies and changes, but each time we end up with a hearty, healthy soup that could have otherwise ended up in the bin.

SPICY SCRAP SOUP

700g frozen scraps (potato peel, parsnip peel, carrot peel, broccoli/cauliflower stalks, you get the idea…)

1 tablespoon chilli flakes

3 tablespoons onion granules

2 tablespoons garlic granules

2 tablespoons salt

2 lemons, juice and zest

7g dried coriander (that's a whole jar)

2 litres of vegetable stock

1 slice of bread

Tip out the frozen peelings into a large stock pot.

Add the chilli flakes, onion and garlic granules, the salt, lemon and dried coriander.

Add the stock and rip slices of the bread into the pan. The bread is what gives it a lovely creamy texture.

Pop the pan on a high heat and bring everything to a rapid boil. As soon as it has boiled lower the heat and leave on a medium heat. With the lid on, leave it to cook for at least 1½ to 2 hours till everything in the pan is soft and falling apart. By this point it should start to look less like peelings.

Take it off the heat and blitz using a stick blender till you have a smooth soup. If you're eating this or making it for the family, pat yourself on the back for making soup – hot, delicious and nutritious – out of peelings, food waste, potential compost. A wholesome meal. If you're serving this to friends, ask them what they think went into it. I reckon they won't be able to guess!

To serve, add a dollop of Greek yoghurt and small sprinkling of freshly scissored chives.

Once cooled, it can be portioned and frozen.

SERVES: 8   ACTIVE TIME: 10 MINUTES   TOTAL TIME: 2 HOURS

Instant noodles are my favourite thing when I need comfort food – they're easy, simple to make and so versatile. They can be eaten as they are or jazzed up to be a bit more special, either with extra chilli sauce or bulked up with some vegetables. By making my own, I'm never short of noodles when I run out of the foil packet variety. I've given the ingredients for four variations – these are the ones I enjoy the most, using up things I tend to have at home. You'll need a selection of 500ml jars with lids – each variation makes one jar. And get your scales out, because we're making a big batch of spice paste to last.

INSTANT NOODLES

For the spice paste

3 medium onions, quartered

2 bulbs of garlic, peeled

100ml vegetable oil

125ml balsamic vinegar

150ml fish sauce

150ml light soy sauce

100g brown sugar

200g chilli paste

For the noodles

40g noodles (per portion) of your choice (you can also buy instant noodles that don't need boiling)

To make the spice paste, blitz the onions and garlic until pulsed but not a smooth paste.

Put the oil into a pan on a medium heat. When it's hot, add the onions and garlic and cook for 10–15 minutes, until the onions are brown. Now add the vinegar, fish sauce, soy sauce, brown sugar and chilli paste, and cook until the mixture is a thick paste with no liquid. This should take about 20 minutes on a medium to low heat.

When the spice paste is cooked and cooled, put it into a jar – it should keep in the fridge for 2 months.

Now to make the noodles. Put a tablespoon of the spice paste into a 500ml jar, along with your portion of noodles and all the other bits. Leave it in the fridge, and when you are ready to eat, pour 300ml of boiling water into the jar and pop the lid on. I like my noodles brothy, but if you like a drier noodle, just add less water. These are great for home but also perfect for taking to work.

continued over page ➡

SERVES: 1 PERSON; PASTE
MAKES ENOUGH FOR 4–8   TOTAL TIME: 35 MINUTES

NOODLE VARIATIONS

CHICKEN AND PEA

1 tablespoon spice paste (see p. 78) + 3 tablespoons frozen peas + 3 table-spoons frozen onions + a small handful of cooked chicken + ¼ of a lime, squeezed, then dropped into the jar + 1 teaspoon dried dill

BEEF AND KIMCHI

1 tablespoon spice paste + 1 spring onion, sliced + 1 tablespoon kimchi + 2 strips of beef jerky, thinly cut with scissors + ½ teaspoon smoked paprika

SOYA MUSHROOM

1 tablespoon spice paste + ½ x 285g tin of sliced mushrooms, drained + 4 tablespoons soya mince, dried or frozen + 1 cube of frozen spinach + a slice of lemon, squeezed and dropped into the jar

EGG NOODLES

1 tablespoon spice paste + 4 tablespoons mixed frozen veg + 2 eggs, cracked straight into the jar + 1 tablespoon coriander seeds, crushed + 1 teaspoon dried dill

While pastry is perhaps my favourite part of a quiche, occasionally, for me, removing one element of a dish makes life just a little bit quicker but still delicious all the same. I love making this because for the most part I have all the ingredients at home. Full of spinach, it fills me with joy – as does anything bright green. It's good eaten straight away, but is even better chilled and eaten later.

CRUSTLESS SPINACH QUICHE

butter, for greasing

100g frozen spinach, defrosted

1 teaspoon ginger paste

1 teaspoon chilli flakes

½ teaspoon salt

¼ teaspoon ground turmeric

150g mature Cheddar cheese, grated

6 eggs, beaten

400ml whole milk

yoghurt, to serve

Preheat the oven to 220°C/fan 200°C. Generously grease a 25cm pie dish.

Put the spinach into a medium bowl, first squeezing out any excess water by pressing it between two sheets of kitchen paper. Mix in the ginger paste, chilli flakes, salt and turmeric, then add the cheese, eggs and milk and mix well, using a fork as this helps separate the spinach.

Pour into the prepared dish and bake in the oven for 30–35 minutes. You will know it is cooked when there is no longer a wobble in the centre.

Take out of the oven and leave for at least 15 minutes before cutting – this will give it just enough time to set, making it easier to cut. I like to serve it simply with some yoghurt.

SERVES: 4–6   ACTIVE TIME: 20 MINUTES   TOTAL TIME: 1 HOUR

To be totally honest you can make anything taste good if you add salty cheese and melted sugar, but when you do the two together, it becomes a taste explosion in your mouth. This is bread topped with an easy chilli pecan paste that can be used in so many different ways, but the paste spread on some bread and topped with slices of Brie, sprinkled with sugar and then grilled, is yummy. Make the paste and you can use it on other things, but first try it with some crunchy sweet grilled Brie.

PECAN BRIE BRÛLÉE

200g pecans

5 tablespoons vegetable oil

4 teaspoons chilli paste

1 teaspoon garlic granules

a pinch of salt

4 slices of bread (sourdough would be nice)

200g Brie cheese

2 tablespoons demerara sugar

To make the pecan chilli paste, put the pecans into a food processor and blitz until totally ground. Gradually add the oil – the mixture should begin to come together. Now add the chilli paste, garlic granules and salt.

Turn the grill to high.

Spread half the chilli pecan paste in an even layer over the bread slices and put them on a baking tray. Cut the Brie into slices and put them on top of the pecan paste. Sprinkle over the sugar and place under the grill until it has caramelized. This should only take 5 minutes, but it can vary depending on your grill/oven.

Put the remainder of the chilli pecan paste into a jar. It will keep in the fridge for up to a month. You can use it on toast or biscuits – I enjoy it spread on salty crackers when I'm peckish in the middle of the night. Or see below for how to use it as a sauce for a delicious chicken dish.

PECAN CHILLI CHICKEN WITH RICE

Mix the leftover paste with 300ml cream, along with the zest and juice of 2 limes. Cook 2 chicken breasts in a pan with some oil, and as soon as the chicken is browned all over, add the nut cream mixture and cook with the lid on for 10 minutes on a low heat. Perfect with some steamed veg or a packet of microwave rice.

SERVES: 4   TOTAL TIME: 20 MINUTES

Aubergines are totally delicious, but I always think they feel like more faff than they are worth when you watch them being salted, left to drain, etc. Mum always just threw them into a curry, but there is a faster way to eat them. The microwave is my friend – you can cook them in the little box of wonder and this is how. The sauce is really versatile, too.

ASIAN AUBERGINE WEDGES

50ml dark soy sauce

2 tablespoons balsamic vinegar

2 tablespoons vegetable oil

1 teaspoon garlic paste

1 teaspoon ginger paste

1 teaspoon chilli paste or gochujang paste

2 tablespoons honey

2 medium aubergines

To serve

a small handful of fresh coriander, chopped

1 red chilli, thinly sliced

1 tablespoon sesame seeds

Start by making the marinade. Put the soy sauce, balsamic, oil, garlic paste, ginger paste, chilli paste and honey into a microwaveable medium-sized bowl.

Remove the stalks from the aubergines, then cut each one into 8 wedges. Throw them all into the bowl of marinade and toss them around. If you can bear it, leave the aubergines to sit and soak up the mixture for at least 5 minutes. You can wait and watch, or make a cup of tea, or chop the coriander and chilli.

Cover the bowl with clingfilm and cook in the microwave on your highest setting for 13 minutes.

When the bowl comes out it will be hot, so be careful. Carefully remove the clingfilm and put the aubergines on a plate. Sprinkle over the coriander, chilli and sesame seeds.

I would normally set aside whatever is left over and use it as part of a salad the next day – you could do that, or you could eat it all now.

STIR-FRIED NOODLES

You can also use this marinade as a stir-fry sauce for noodles or serve it with egg-fried rice. Cook 2 nests of noodles following the packet instructions. Drain, then return the noodles to the saucepan with the aubergine sauce and cook for 1–2 minutes, tossing to coat the noodles.

SERVES: 2–4   ACTIVE TIME: 10 MINUTES   TOTAL TIME: 25 MINUTES

Chicken breast can be dry and it's not always my favourite protein of choice – bit of lamb any day! But enough sauce can really transform it, and packing the marinara with lots of flavour is important. Also, this is my creamy version mixed with hummus, because I always have a stray tub at the end of the week, and it works beautifully in this. We're going to make a double batch here, so that you have another meal for 4 in the freezer, but if you prefer to just make enough for today, simply halve all of the ingredients.

CREAMY MARINARA CHICKEN

For the chicken

8 chicken breasts

500g passata

1 tablespoon onion granules

1 tablespoon dried basil

1 tablespoon dried oregano

1½ teaspoons salt

1 teaspoon black pepper

½ x 198g jar of capers (about 65g capers, drained weight)

3 tablespoons olive oil

2 tablespoons hummus

For the couscous

1 medium courgette, grated

400g couscous

1 chicken stock cube, crushed

1 x 400g tin of chickpeas, drained

2 tablespoons basil pesto

100ml olive oil

Cut a horizontal slit in each chicken breast, then tease open to allow lots of space for sauce. Just make sure you don't cut all the way through. Place 4 breasts in one casserole dish and 4 in the other, making sure one of the dishes is freezer-safe.

Preheat the oven to 220°C/fan 200°C.

Put the passata, onion granules, basil, oregano, salt and black pepper into a bowl. Squeeze any excess moisture out of the capers and chop them roughly, then add them to the bowl along with the oil and hummus. Divide the mixture between the two casserole dishes, then get your hands in to encourage the mixture to get deep into those slits.

Cover one dish and pop it into the freezer. Place the other one in the oven and bake for 25–30 minutes.

Meanwhile prepare the couscous by grating the courgette into a big bowl. Pour in the couscous, crush in the stock cube, then pour in boiling water until it reaches just 1cm above the couscous line. Cover with clingfilm and set aside.

Drain the chickpeas, then pop them into a small bowl and stir in the pesto and oil. Once all the water has been absorbed into the couscous, fluff it up with a fork, then add all the chickpeas and mix really well. By now the chicken should be ready.

Put half the couscous into a freezer bag and leave to cool before freezing.

Now it's time for lunch.

I only recently discovered through the powers of social media that you can eat a kiwi with the skin on! I mean, why didn't I think of that? We eat peaches with their fuzzy skin and don't bat an eyelid, even if the sensation is that of licking a Russian Blue! Kiwis are a great balance of tart and sweet with the added pop of the little black crunchy seeds that make it much more than a lunchbox snack. This is a welcome change to a potato salad at a barbecue.

KIWI SALAD

5 tablespoons olive oil

5 tablespoons lemon juice

3 tablespoons runny honey

1 clove of garlic, finely grated

1 tablespoon za'atar

4 tablespoons tahini

1 red onion, peeled and finely diced

8 kiwis, firm but not overripe, topped and tailed and chopped into chunks, skins and all!

1 cucumber

200g feta crumbled or roughly chopped

a small handful of fresh dill, finely chopped

2 tablespoons black sesame seeds

Start by making the dressing at the bottom of a large serving bowl. Saves on washing-up if nothing else. Add the oil, lemon juice, honey, garlic, za'atar and tahini and mix.

Now add the onion and mix through really well. The onion will soften as it sits in the vinegar. Now add the kiwi.

To prepare the cucumber, slice lengthways and remove the seeds using a teaspoon. Cut into long strips and cube. Add to the bowl. Add the feta on top and sprinkle over the chopped dill and sesame seeds.

Don't mix the salad till you are ready to serve, or everything will wilt and go weird.

I discovered these in the frozen veg aisle and I have not looked back since. They are a great alternative to peas but firmer, less sweet, and simply delicious. So it's worth having a bag in the freezer, especially if you, like me, are not a huge pea fan … unless they're mushy.

EDAMAME WILD RICE SALAD

300g cottage cheese

7-8cm piece of ginger, peeled

½ teaspoon salt

4 tablespoons olive oil

2 tablespoons honey

1 lemon, juice and zest

30g fresh parsley, leaves removed from the stalks

4 tablespoons pickled red cabbage

250g precooked wild rice (or precooked rice of your choice), cooled

600g frozen edamame beans, cooked and cooled

In a large serving bowl, add the cottage cheese and grate in the ginger.

Add the salt, oil and honey, then the zest and juice of the lemon and mix really well.

Add the parsley leaves. I don't like chopping them up because I think parsley is so subtle it can almost be used as a leafy alternative in a salad. Keep the stalks, they would work well chopped into a chicken soup. Freeze in a bag, keeping the stalks whole.

Now add the pickled red cabbage and the rice. Add the cooled edamame beans and mix through.

SERVES: 4–8   TOTAL TIME: 15 MINUTES

Jackets are my favourite lunch, simply with some beans and cheese. Or even just a knob of butter, seasoned well with some black pepper. But I like to make these when I have a little more time to spare. They are delicious and moist, with cottage cheese running through them, topped with sriracha and cheese. I've also included some of my other favourite filling options on the next page if you fancy something different – or why not do a combination if there are a few of you?

COTTAGE CHEESE AND ONION POTATO SKINS

8 medium potatoes

1 small red onion, finely chopped

1 teaspoon garlic paste

300g full-fat cottage cheese

½ teaspoon paprika

½ teaspoon salt, plus more for sprinkling

a few tablespoons oil

sriracha sauce, whichever is your favourite flavour (I like the green top)

100g red Leicester cheese, freshly grated or frozen (I always have some in the freezer)

bunch of spring onions, chopped, as optional garnish

Start by microwaving the potatoes. Prick them with a fork (so they don't explode), then lay them on their sides and microwave for 10 minutes. Turn them over and microwave again for another 10 minutes.

Meanwhile, put the red onion, garlic paste, cottage cheese, paprika and salt into a bowl and give it a really good stir.

Preheat the oven to 220°C/fan 200°C.

As soon as the potatoes are ready, put them on to 2 baking trays, big enough to hold them all when they are cut in half. Drizzle them with oil and sprinkle generously with salt. This will give them a crisp skin. As soon as the potatoes are cool enough to handle, slice them in half lengthways, then scoop out the flesh and put it into a bowl, being careful not to pierce the skins. Lay the skins back on the baking trays ready to fill.

Mash the potato flesh and mix in the cottage cheese mixture. Spoon this mixture back into the potato skins. Drizzle over the sriracha and sprinkle on the cheese. Bake in the oven for 20 minutes, until the cheese is bubbling and golden. Sprinkle with chopped spring onions (if you like) and serve.

Any leftovers can be frozen uncovered until they are firm, then wrapped individually in foil.

SERVES: 8 (MAKES 16 HALVES)   ACTIVE TIME: 30 MINUTES   TOTAL TIME: 1 HOUR 15 MINUTES

POTATO SKINS FIVE WAYS

Here are some other filling variations for potato skins – the method is the same as on p. 90. Just mix the filling with the mashed potato, fill the skins, and top with cheese.

BACON + BEAN

1 x 400g tin of baked beans + 1 teaspoon smoked paprika + ½ teaspoon salt + 4 bacon rashers (turkey or vegetarian rashers work equally well), popped into a microwave for 1 minute, then thinly snipped with scissors + 75g mature Cheddar cheese, for the top

PESTO

3 tablespoons pesto + 200g feta cheese, crumbled + 75g mature Cheddar cheese, for the top

CHILLI

1 x 392g tin of chilli con carne + 1 teaspoon chilli flakes + 1 tablespoon Worcestershire sauce + 150ml sour cream, mixed with 75g mature Cheddar cheese for the top before baking

BOMBAY MIX

3 tablespoons curry paste + 1 green chilli, finely chopped + fresh coriander, finely chopped + Bombay mix plus 75g mature Cheddar cheese, for the top

CORONATION TUNA

See p. 96

I grew up eating rice for every single meal, but I don't eat it as often now unless I'm at my mum's. But there is something so comforting about eating a lunch cooked in a big pot that really fills a gap. This rice dish is no exception. It's salty and sweet and perfect with prawns. Best of all, once you have made this pot for lunch, you have a second lot that can be frozen for dinner another day. I like to eat mine with a poached or fried egg – any situation where there is a runny warm egg adds to the deliciousness. Sprinkle some chopped red chilli on top too, if you like.

PRAWN MALAY RICE

5 tablespoons vegetable oil

3 tablespoons garlic paste

2 small onions, chopped

1 teaspoon salt

5 tablespoons soy sauce

4 tablespoons runny honey

1 teaspoon chilli powder

1 tablespoon curry powder

1.5 litres boiling water

750g basmati rice

325g cooked king prawns

200g frozen peas

fried eggs (optional)

Put the oil into a large non-stick pan and turn the heat up to high. Add the garlic paste, followed quickly by the onions and salt. Give it a good stir to make sure that the onions don't burn too much, and keep them moving and browning.

Lower the heat completely, and add the soy sauce, honey, chilli powder and curry powder, and cook for a minute on a medium heat.

Have the hot water at the ready. Add the rice to the pan and turn up the heat, stirring all the time. As you stir you will see the rice become white in the heat of the pan.

Now stir in the prawns. Pour in the water and keep stirring the rice on a high heat. As soon as the liquid has thickened, and the rice is more noticeable, add the peas, give it all a final stir and pop the lid on. Turn the heat down to the lowest setting and let it steam for at least 15 minutes.

Fluff the rice up with a spoon and leave to stand with the lid off for a few minutes before serving. Eat as is, or fry a few eggs while you wait for it to cool a little.

Freeze leftovers in a bag or tub once the rice is completely cool.

SERVES: 6   ACTIVE TIME: 30 MINUTES   TOTAL TIME: 45 MINUTES

Coronation chicken sandwiches seemed a bizarre concept to me. I never found a halal one that I could try, but the colour and the distinct lack of curryness made me suspicious. But I love how some things stand the test of time, and now this is one of my faves and it works really well with tuna. With very little fishy flavour, it absorbs all the deliciousness of the Coronation flavours. I make enough of this so that I can make 2 sandwiches – one for me and one for the other half while we are on our lunch break. And I leave the rest of the tuna mix in the fridge for a salad or, better still, to top a hot jacket potato, with some extra baby spinach.

CORONATION TUNA

3 x 145g tins of tuna chunks in brine, drained

½ teaspoon ground cinnamon

1 teaspoon ground black pepper

1 heaped teaspoon curry powder, mild or hot, as you prefer

2 tablespoons mango chutney

2 tablespoons raisins

a pinch of salt

10–12 tablespoons full-fat mayonnaise (I like it creamier and have been known to go heavier, but this is entirely up to you)

To serve

4 slices of brown bread

butter, for spreading

baby spinach leaves

Put the tuna into a Tupperware container with a lid, making sure to drain off any excess moisture first. Nobody wants a soggy filling. (I'm mixing this in the Tupperware to save on washing up.) Add the cinnamon, black pepper, curry powder, mango chutney and raisins, along with a pinch of salt, and give it all a good mix until well combined.

Add the mayonnaise. I like a very creamy filling, so if by the time you get to 8 spoons, and you think you have enough, that's totally up to you. I for one can keep going. Mix well.

Butter both slices of bread and layer on your tuna filling. Add the spinach and sandwich together.

Before you tuck in, close up your Tupperware and save the leftovers for another lunch during the week. You might like to use it as a filling for potato skins (see p. 92).

I cook the tortellini in the vegetable stock rather than boiling them separately – as the bits of filled pasta boil in the stock, they thicken the sauce, giving you a warming soup. And more than anything else, it saves on washing up. Everything that goes into this recipe uses up bits in jars and bits from the freezer, which means you can have a nice wholesome warm lunch with as little prep as possible.

ONE-POT TORTELLINI

1 litre boiling water

2 vegetable stock cubes

1 teaspoon salt

½ teaspoon ground turmeric

1 teaspoon garlic granules

1 teaspoon chilli flakes

100g frozen peas

190g jarred asparagus, drained and roughly chopped

600g filled tortellini

a large handful of fresh mint, chopped

1 lime, juice and zest

1 tablespoon butter

Bring the water to the boil in a saucepan on a medium heat, then add the stock cubes and stir until dissolved. Add the salt, turmeric, garlic granules, chilli flakes and peas.

Add the chopped asparagus, along with the tortellini, and allow to gently boil for 5 minutes. Add the chopped mint and the lime juice and zest and take off the heat. Stir in the butter and let it melt. Then it's ready to eat.

As soon as it has cooled, if you want to, you can portion out into freezer-safe, microwave-safe pots with lids and freeze.

Bread dipped in egg and fried is a winner any which way, and this is a little bit different from its sweet counterparts. I don't see why we can't have French toast for lunch instead of, or including, breakfast. It's great having these in the freezer, too, for those days when you don't have time to think about what to make for lunch. You can just pop them in the oven to reheat while you're getting on with other things.

SAVOURY FRENCH TOAST

6 eggs

100ml whole milk

½ teaspoon salt

2 teaspoons sugar

¼ teaspoon ground turmeric

1 teaspoon garlic granules

1 teaspoon onion granules

6 slices of sliced white bread

3 slices of cooked ham/
    turkey/vegetarian
    ham slices

3 slices of mild cheese

vegetable oil, for frying

Put the eggs into a shallow bowl, wide enough to take a slice of bread, and add the milk, salt, sugar, turmeric, garlic granules and onion granules. Mix well and leave to sit for 5 minutes, allowing the granules to rehydrate in the egg mix.

Sandwich the slices of bread together with the ham and cheese. Dip them into the egg mixture and pop them on a plate.

Put a non-stick frying pan on the hob with a thin layer of oil on the base. Take one of the sandwiches and dip it back into the egg mixture to get another soaking, then fry on a medium heat for 3 minutes, until it has a golden colour and the cheese begins to melt. Turn over and cook for another 3 minutes, pressing lightly with a spatula to help seal the bread, then pop the sandwich on to a plate lined with some kitchen paper. When they're all done, cut them in half.

Add some more oil to the base of the pan and repeat with the other sandwiches, dipping and frying in the same way. Depending how absorbent the bread is, you may find you have enough eggy mix left to make another sandwich.

Serve hot, with a dollop of ketchup if you like.

These are best eaten fresh, but if there are any left over you can wrap them in foil and freeze them.

SERVES: 6 HALVES, SERVES 3   TOTAL TIME: 25 MINUTES

I don't know about you, but we always have baked beans in the cupboard so this is a great recipe for if you want to try something different with them. It might sound unusual . . . you're just going to have to trust me on this one! If you also like coleslaw, double up the sauce ingredients in green and pop the extra ingredients on your shopping list.

BAKED BEAN FALAFEL

For the falafel

4 x 400g tins of baked beans

1 large egg

6 cloves of garlic, crushed

1 large onion, chopped

1 teaspoon salt

1 teaspoon chilli powder

1 tablespoon ground cumin

1 tablespoon ground
    coriander

120g chickpea flour

a large handful of fresh
    parsley, finely chopped

cooking oil spray

For the sauce

1 clove of garlic, grated

1 teaspoon salt

4 tablespoons mayonnaise

a squeeze of lemon juice

1 tablespoon chopped fresh
    parsley

2 tablespoons sriracha sauce

Coleslaw (optional extra)

3 carrots, grated

½ white cabbage, finely
    shredded

½ red cabbage, finely
    shredded

1 red onion, thinly sliced

Drain the beans, keeping the sauce aside in a separate bowl, then rinse the beans and leave them to drain. Put the beans and the egg into a blender and whiz until you have a smooth paste. Transfer to a bowl and add the garlic, onion, salt, chilli powder, cumin and coriander. Add the chickpea flour and mix everything together – it may be quite a wet mix.

Preheat the oven to 220°C/fan 200°C and have a large baking tray ready, generously greased.

Using wet hands, create walnut-sized balls of the bean mixture and pop them on the tray. Spray them with oil all over and bake in the oven for 25–30 minutes, turning them halfway through.

To make the sauce, add the garlic, salt, mayonnaise, lemon juice, parsley and sriracha to 150g of the drained bean sauce from the tin. Stir and set aside.

If you don't want to waste the rest of the bean juice, double up the sauce ingredients to make a double batch of it. Use half as a dipping sauce for the falafel. Stir the other half through the coleslaw ingredients listed.

When the falafels are baked I like to eat them squashed inside a soft bap, smothered with the sauce and some salad (and some of the coleslaw, if you've made it). There is plenty here to eat and to freeze, so pop the extras into a freezer bag.

The coleslaw will keep in the fridge for 2-3 days. Serve alongside cold cuts of meat, or in a jacket potato.

Make a coleslaw at the same time as the Baked Bean Falafel (see p. 100) and you have the perfect accompaniment for many other dishes.

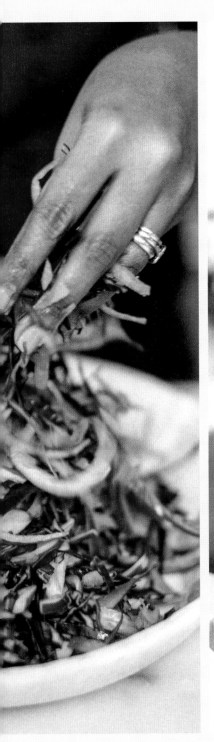

I didn't grow up eating cheese or with it being around the house. It's very not Bengali of me when I pick cheese and crackers over a curry, but there you go. This Indian cheese is like halloumi, creamy yet it doesn't melt. It's great for absorbing flavours and takes on the deliciousness of anything you put with it. Best of all it can be frozen, so it means I have spicy cheese on tap. I am making enough filling here to fill 6 pockets, with some left over to either freeze, or add to pasta to make a delicious pasta salad. When you have double quantities, you have done the hard work once and you can decide later how to eat it, again!

PANEER PITTA

4 tablespoons vegetable oil, plus a dash

2 x 250g packs of paneer, cubed

2 tablespoons garlic paste

1 large red onion, sliced

1 teaspoon salt

1 tablespoon tomato purée

2 large red peppers, thinly sliced

1 teaspoon ground cumin

1 teaspoon chilli flakes

1 tablespoon runny honey

1 lemon, juice and zest

fresh coriander, chopped

85g watercress, roughly chopped

3 pitta breads

Start by putting the oil into a non-stick frying pan on a high heat. Add the cubes of paneer and fry, making sure to stir occasionally so that the cheese turns golden brown – not only does this add to the flavour, but it also creates a texture that the sauce can adhere to. Fry for about 5 minutes then transfer to a plate.

Add another small dash of oil and lower the heat to medium. Add the garlic paste and cook for a minute, then add the sliced red onions and salt and cook for a few minutes, until the onions are soft.

Squeeze in the tomato purée and cook for a minute. Add a few splashes of cold water to stop it sticking, that's all. Throw in the peppers, cumin and chilli flakes and cook for another 10 minutes with the lid on, until the peppers are soft and limp.

Pour in the honey, then add the juice and zest of the lemon and the paneer and cook on a high heat for 2–3 minutes. The mixture should be dry and the cubes of cheese should be coated with the sauce.

Take off the heat, then stir in the coriander and watercress – the cress does not need cooking, it will wilt from the heat of everything else surrounding it yet maintain some of its fire.

Halve the pitta breads and toast them, then fill with the mixture.

Pop the filling you have left over into a Tupperware container and, when it is totally cool, freeze it or stick it in the fridge for later (or see opposite for how to make a pasta salad out of it).

PANEER PASTA SALAD

This is a great way of using up any leftovers you have of that tasty cheese without having to serve it exactly the same way. Mix 300g of cooked and cooled pasta with the left-over paneer. Add ½ a chopped cucumber and a small bag of watercress. Stir in a few tablespoons of yoghurt, mix well, and you have a really simple pasta salad.

Chow mein is the easiest thing to order, but even easier to make. I love the flavours of honey mustard, so I'm keeping it simple. I also whip-up a double batch and skewer half the chicken for the freezer, so if I have to make a quick lunch or need something to whack on a grill, I have the same honey mustard chicken, minus the chow mein. If you don't want the extra in the freezer, simply halve the ingredients in green.

HONEY MUSTARD CHOW MEIN

10 chicken thighs, thinly sliced

4 tablespoons runny honey

4 tablespoons wholegrain mustard

4 cloves of garlic, minced

a 2.5cm piece of ginger, peeled and grated

4 tablespoons soy sauce

1 teaspoon salt

3 tablespoons sriracha sauce

oil, for frying

2 medium onions, thinly sliced

450g stir-fry vegetables

275g ready-made noodles

a large handful of fresh coriander

50g salted peanuts, roughly chopped

wedges of lime

Put the chicken thighs into a large bowl with the honey, mustard, garlic, ginger, soy sauce, salt and sriracha, and leave to marinate.

Place a large non-stick frying pan or wok on the hob on a high heat. Add the oil and, when it's really hot, add the onions. When they are very brown, add half the marinated chicken, putting the other half into the fridge for later.

Continue cooking the chicken on a high heat, and when it is cooked through, add the stir-fry veg and the noodles and mix together, before lowering to a medium heat for 5 minutes or until the vegetables are just a little bit soft, but still crisp.

Take off the heat, sprinkle with the coriander and peanuts, and serve with a wedge of lime – and I'm always tempted to add another dash of sriracha.

Once you have eaten, put the marinated chicken from the fridge on to skewers and pop on to a tray to freeze. When frozen, take the skewers off the tray and put them into a bag to store.

CHICKEN SKEWERS

If you have made a double batch of chicken put half of the marinated meat on to skewers and pop on a tray to freeze. When frozen, take the skewers off the tray and put them into a freezer bag to store.

Defrost fully when needed, then cook in a preheated oven (220°C/ fan 200°C) for 30 minutes, turning halfway through.

SERVES: 4   TOTAL TIME: 40 MINUTES

As the kids get bigger, they seem to get busier, with social calendars that make my schedule look as bare as my cupboards on a Saturday evening before a weekly shop. So this is just another really easy way to make a hot sandwich that is transportable, warm and yummy. One of these days I will be partying as much as my kids – not any time soon though.

CORNED BEEF SUB

3 tablespoons vegetable oil

2 cloves of garlic, crushed

1 large onion, diced

½ teaspoon salt

1 red pepper, diced

2 medium potatoes, peeled and diced into 1cm pieces

½ teaspoon ground turmeric

½ teaspoon chilli powder

1 lemon, zest and juice

2 x 340g tins of corned beef, diced into 1cm pieces

4 sub rolls

150g Gouda cheese, grated

To serve

sriracha sauce

rocket or lettuce

Heat the oil in a large non-stick frying pan, then add the garlic and onions and cook for a few minutes until soft and translucent. Add the salt and cook until the onions are a golden brown.

Add the red pepper and potatoes and cook with a lid on for 10 minutes. If it starts to stick, add a small splash of water to create some steam for the potatoes to cook.

Now mix in the turmeric, chilli powder and lemon zest and juice. Stir in the corned beef and continue to cook on a medium heat.

Preheat the oven to 190°C/fan 170°C.

As soon as the potatoes are tender, take the pan off the heat. Lay the four sub rolls, sliced and open, on a baking tray and fill one half of each with the corned beef mixture in an even layer. Sprinkle over the cheese and bake in the oven until it has melted.

Take out and drizzle with sriracha, then fill with rocket or lettuce and close the rolls up.

If you have any filling left over it can be frozen, then thawed and used again in the same way. Or, for a traditional corned beef hash breakfast, add a couple of dashes of Worcestershire sauce when reheating, stir in some chopped parsley and serve with a fried egg on top.

SERVES: 4   ACTIVE TIME: 15 MINUTES   TOTAL TIME: 40 MINUTES

These cloud breads are so light it's like eating air, but delicious air. I like making them but I also like topping them – they are great carriers of strong flavours. Without the topping, the breads can be used as carb-free pizza bases or burger buns, or can be toasted and eaten with butter and jam. The fish mix also makes a great filling for an omelette – or into a showstopping tart.

CLOUD BREAD WITH CREAMY MACKEREL TOPPING

For the bread

cooking oil spray

4 large eggs, separated

50g full-fat cream cheese

¼ teaspoon cream of tartar

For the topping

100g cream cheese

3 tablespoons whole milk

1 teaspoon nigella seeds

2 spring onions, finely
  chopped

a squeeze of lemon juice

salt, to taste

250g hot smoked mackerel
  fillets, flaked

Preheat the oven to 150°C/fan 130°C. Grease and line two baking trays.

Whisk the egg whites to stiff peaks. Using the same whisk, in a different bowl whisk the yolks with the cream cheese and cream of tartar. Add the whisked egg whites a little at a time until the mixture is well incorporated. There will be lumps, but that is normal.

Take large spoonfuls of the mixture and make 4 or 5 rounds per tray, making sure they are not touching. Bake in the oven for 20 minutes. While that's happening, make the topping by mixing the cream cheese with the milk, nigella seeds, spring onions, lemon juice and a sprinkle of salt. Stir in the flakes of mackerel.

As soon as the first batch comes out of the oven, they are ready to be lightly topped with the creamy fish mixture. Take them off the tray and leave to cool completely.

Make the rest of the cloud bread in the same way. If the remaining mixture separates while the first batch is baking, just give it a stir to bring it back together.

CREAMY MACKEREL TART

You can add 2 eggs and 3 tablespoons of double cream to the fish mix and use it as a tart filling. Line an 18cm tart tin with 300g of shortcrust pastry, then add a sheet of baking paper and some baking beads. Bake in the oven at 180°C/fan 160°C for 20 minutes, then remove the beads and bake for another 5 minutes. Spoon in the filling, then reduce the temperature to 160°C/fan 140°C and bake for a further 25 minutes.

MAKES: 8–10   ACTIVE TIME: 20 MINUTES   TOTAL TIME: 1 HOUR

I love a tart – they are simple to make, feel impressive and the flavour possibilities are endless. The filling for this is so good that I've come up with some other ways you can use it. Double the ingredients in green if you want to make a curry or a soup at the same time – see opposite.

SWEET POTATO AND GOAT'S CHEESE TART

For the pastry

300g plain flour

a pinch of salt

150g cold butter, cubed

3–4 tablespoons
   cold water

For the filling

2 tablespoons vegetable
   oil

2 cloves of garlic, crushed

1 large sprig of fresh
   thyme

2 small red onions, sliced

½ teaspoon salt

1 large sweet potato,
   peeled and cut into
   1cm cubes (about 300g)

100g goat's cheese

3 medium eggs

200g crème fraîche

½ teaspoon salt

1 teaspoon paprika

For the dressing

85g watercress

1 lemon, zest and juice

100g pine nuts

5 tablespoons olive oil

a pinch of salt

Start by making the pastry. Put the flour and salt into a bowl, then add the butter and rub it into the flour until it resembles breadcrumbs. Add a tablespoon of water at a time until the dough comes together.

Dust a work surface with flour and roll out the pastry until it is large enough to cover the base and sides of a deep 23cm loose-bottomed tart tin and leave a 1cm overhang. Prick the base a few times, then pop the tart shell into the freezer for 15 minutes. Preheat the oven to 200°C/fan 180°C.

Now make the filling. Heat the oil in a pan, then add the garlic and cook until golden – this should only take a few minutes. Add the thyme sprig, along with the onions and salt, and cook until the onions are soft. Stir in the sweet potatoes, then pop the pan on a low to medium heat and cover to allow the potatoes to soften. This should take about 10 minutes.

Take the tart shell out of the freezer. Put a piece of baking paper inside, with some baking beads, and bake in the oven for 15 minutes.

The sweet potatoes should be cooked by now, so take them off the heat and leave to cool a little. Discard the thyme sprig, but leave the little leaves in there.

Make the dressing by whizzing together the watercress, lemon zest and juice, pine nuts, oil and salt.

Take the tart shell out of the oven, remove the paper and beads, and bake for another 5 minutes. Take it out, and reduce the oven temperature to 180°C/fan 160°C.

Spoon the potato mixture into the tart shell and scatter the chunks of goat's cheese all over.

Put the eggs, crème fraîche, salt and paprika into a bowl and mix until well combined. Pour into the tart shell, dot a few teaspoons of the dressing over the top, and bake in the oven for 30–35 minutes.

Use the rest of the dressing to toss through a simple green salad mixed with tomatoes, or as a dressing for Hasselback Squash (see p. 180).

Leave the tart in the tin for 10 minutes, then trim the edges. Leave it in the tin for another 30 minutes before taking it out. Serve the tart warm or chilled.

Any leftovers can be kept in the fridge for 3 days or frozen.

SWEET POTATO AND GOAT'S CHEESE CURRY

You can also make a great curry by adding a few extra ingredients. Add a large glug of vegetable oil to a large pan and heat over a medium heat. Add two red onions, chopped into large chunks. As soon as the onions are soft, add 4 generous tablespoons of curry paste (see p. 240) and heat through. Add two large sweet potatoes (peeled and diced) to the pan and give everything a good mix. Add 500ml hot water and leave to simmer over a low to medium heat, with the lid on, for 25 minutes, making sure to check and stir occasionally. As soon as the potatoes are tender, take off the heat and stir some chopped watercress through. Sprinkle over some pine nuts and serve with a dollop of yoghurt and some naan on the side.

SWEET POTATO AND GOAT'S CHEESE SOUP

The filling works great as a soup, and for that I double the first 7 filling ingredients and blend them with 500ml of vegetable stock. This makes 4 servings and can be frozen or stored in the fridge for 3 days. Garnish with your choice of herbs. I use thyme, watercress, some paprika and a splash of olive oil. You can also add some of the leftover dressing, some extra pine nuts and a crumbling of goat's cheese.

The filling for the Goat's Cheese Tart works great as both a soup and as the base of a curry. By adding a few extra ingredients you have two delicious alternatives, perfect if friends pop around, or to store away in the freezer.

Fish burgers are our favourite thing to eat – they're warming and comforting. Imagine all your favourite foods in burger form! Well, that's a challenge if ever I heard one. These fish pie patties are all nuzzled inside a soft white bap squished with a pea tartare! Yum. I tend to make my own bread for this recipe, but there's nothing wrong with shop bought if you need to save a little more time. I like to serve them with oven chips alongside.

FISH PIE BURGER

8 white baps (see p. 244 if you'd like to make your own)

For the fish pie patty

700g Maris Piper potatoes, peeled and diced

3 eggs

2 x 340g packets of fish pie mix

300ml water

2 cloves of garlic, grated

1 lemon, zest only (keep juice for the pea tartare)

1 teaspoon salt

1 teaspoon onion salt

1 teaspoon black pepper

a small handful of fresh parsley, finely chopped

½ a bunch of fresh chives, chopped

Put the potatoes into a pan of cold water and bring to the boil, putting the eggs into the pan at the same time. Boil until the potatoes are tender and falling off a knife when tested. Drain, then tip the potatoes into a large bowl and leave the colander in the sink for the fish.

Peel the eggs. Mash the potatoes and leave to cool (I open a window so that the breeze cools them in no time). Grate the eggs straight into the bowl of potatoes.

Pop the fish into a pan with the water, bring to the boil, then leave to simmer for just 5 minutes. Drain the fish in the same colander you used for the potatoes. Once the fish is cool enough to handle, flake it into the bowl of egg and potato.

To shape the fish patties, have a large baking tray ready. Add the garlic, lemon zest, salt, onion salt, pepper, parsley and chives to the bowl of fish and potato, then get your hands in and give it a good mix. Divide the mixture into 8 and shape into patties (you may need to wet your hands to make sure it doesn't all stick to your fingers). Place on the tray and pop into the fridge while you prepare the pea tartare.

For the pea tartare

200g frozen peas, thawed
    and drained

5 heaped tablespoons
    mayonnaise

1 teaspoon mustard powder

1 small onion, finely chopped

a squeeze of lemon juice

a small handful of fresh
    parsley, chopped

a sprinkling of salt

For the coating

200g plain flour

3 eggs, beaten

175g plain breadcrumbs

Put the peas into a bowl of boiling water and leave for a few minutes to defrost, then drain them and pop them into a bowl. Using the back of a fork, just mush them lightly. Stir in the mayo, mustard, onion, lemon juice, parsley and a sprinkling of salt and put to one side.

Put the flour, beaten egg and breadcrumbs on to separate plates. Take the fish patties out of the fridge and dip each one first into the flour, then into the egg, then into the breadcrumbs and put them back on the tray.

If you are making oven chips to go with the fish pie burgers, now's the time to get them in.

Place a medium-sized non-stick frying pan on a medium heat and add 1cm of oil. Have a tray lined with kitchen paper ready. Fry 2 patties at a time, for 2 minutes on each side. Once they are fried, pop them on to the tray while you finish frying the rest.

To make up your burgers, slice the baps across the middle. Add a patty to each one, then a spoonful of the pea tartare, and put the tops of the rolls back on.

If you are only eating a few burgers and want to save some, they can be cooled, wrapped in foil minus the pea tartare, and frozen.

I've seen these poke bowls popping up all over the place, especially when I'm in and around London. I've seen a few at festivals too – it's like they're trying to say, 'Make way, sushi.' These have all the deliciousness of sushi but in a bowl, which means there is more of it. With a sticky rice base, they can be topped with fresh ingredients, or leftovers from the fridge – make it colourful, make it delicious, make it yours. The sauce also makes a great marinade for chicken wings – double the ingredients in green and see below for how to use it.

BLACK PEPPER POKE SALMON BOWL

For the rice

500g sushi rice/sticky rice

2 tablespoons apple cider vinegar

1 teaspoon salt

2 teaspoons sugar

For the sauce

25g mayonnaise

3 teaspoons soy sauce

1 teaspoon sesame oil

½ teaspoon fish sauce

1 tablespoon sriracha sauce

1 lemon, juice only

1 teaspoon black pepper

To finish

2 really fresh skinless salmon fillets (200g), cut into cubes

2 small or 1 large avocado, sliced (with a squeeze of lemon to prevent browning)

4 tablespoons pickled red cabbage

1 large carrot, peeled and grated

a large handful of salted peanuts, roughly chopped

2 spring onions, sliced

sesame seeds

nori sheets, snipped into strips

a sprinkling of black pepper

Start with the rice: place it in a saucepan and wash it until the water runs clear. Add just enough water to come 1cm above the rice. Stirring all the time, place on a high heat (stirring will ensure that the rice doesn't settle on the base). Once it comes to the boil, let it simmer on a medium heat until all the water has evaporated. Pop the lid on and leave on the lowest setting to steam (about 10 minutes).

Meanwhile gather together everything you need to finish off this bowl.

Make the sauce by mixing together the mayo, soy sauce, sesame oil, fish sauce, sriracha, lemon juice and black pepper. Put the salmon into a bowl, then pour over the sauce (half, if you're making chicken wings as well) and mix thoroughly.

Once the rice has steamed, mix the vinegar, salt and sugar in a small bowl, then pour over the rice and stir through.

Divide the rice between two bowls and start adding all the different finishing ingredients. The salmon first, then the avocado, red cabbage, carrot and peanuts. Sprinkle with the spring onions, sesame and nori, add a sprinkling of black pepper, and you're ready to eat.

MARINATED CHICKEN WINGS

Pour the remaining half of the sauce over 1kg chicken wings and mix well to coat. Pop the wings into a freezer bag and leave for another day. To use, defrost fully and bake at 220°C/fan 200°C for 40 minutes, turning half way.

SERVES: 4   ACTIVE TIME: 30 MINUTES   TOTAL TIME: 45 MINUTES

Does 'plate pie' mean it's my plate and all the pie is mine too? This pie is covered in butter pastry and filled with Bombay-style potatoes and corned beef. Not something I was used to eating, but I'm happy to admit I love the stuff now! I always make two of these, one to eat and one to freeze, so double up all the ingredients if you fancy doing that. You can also prepare this in advance and cook it from frozen if you want to save even more time.

CORNED BEEF BOMBAY PIE

For the pastry

450g plain flour, plus extra
  for dusting

a pinch of salt

200g unsalted butter, cubed

a few tablespoons of cold water

1 egg, beaten, for sealing and
  glaze

For the filling

2 tablespoons vegetable oil

1 teaspoon Bengali Spice Mix
  (*Panch Phoran* – see p. 237)

3 cloves of garlic, crushed

1 medium onion, finely chopped

1 celery stick, finely diced

1 teaspoon salt

½ teaspoon ground turmeric

1 teaspoon paprika

1 large potato, peeled and cut
  into 2.5cm cubes

1 carrot, peeled and sliced into
  5mm coins

1 small red pepper, cut into
  1cm dice

100ml water

3 teaspoons tamarind paste

340g corned beef, cut into
  2.5cm cubes

a small handful of fresh coriander,
  roughly chopped

Start with the pastry. Put the flour into a bowl with the salt and rub in the butter until it resembles breadcrumbs. Add the water a little at a time to bring the dough together, and as soon as you have done that, cut off one third of the dough. Wrap both pieces and put into the fridge to chill.

Now to the filling. Put the oil into a medium non-stick pan and add the spice mix. As soon as the seeds start to pop, add the garlic, onion, celery and salt. Cook on a high heat until the onions are soft, then lower the heat, add the turmeric and paprika and cook for another minute. Add the potatoes, carrots, red pepper, water and tamarind and cook for about 20 minutes on a medium heat with the lid on, until the potatoes are cooked. Take off the lid to dry out any extra moisture. Take off the heat, stir in the corned beef and coriander, then transfer to a plate to cool.

Preheat the oven to 220°C/fan 200°C and place a baking tray in it.

Roll out the larger bit of pastry to the thickness of a pound coin, and big enough to cover the base and sides of a 23cm ovenproof plate with a slight overhang. I like to use an enamel plate. Roll out the other piece so it fits the top with a small overhang. Spoon the filling over the pastry, then brush the edges with beaten egg and top with the smaller piece of pastry. Cut off the overhang, crimp the edges and brush the top with egg. Cut a slit in the top to allow steam out, and bake for 30–35 minutes.

When it's ready, leave it to rest for 20 minutes before eating.

If you are preparing this in advance, to be baked at a later date, do everything but the egg wash and place in the freezer. Preheat the oven to 200°C/fan 180°C, pop your egg wash over the frozen pastry then bake from frozen for 45–50 minutes until piping hot all the way through.

A kedgeree to me is a mash-up of flavours in a staple such as rice, topped off with some eggs. I used to have this all the time as a child, because we always had leftover rice. But why not mix things up? The big bold colours in this just make me want to eat it with my eyes before any other sense. You will probably have enough here to freeze some for another day, too.

WATERCRESS QUINOA KEDGEREE

300g quinoa

50ml vegetable stock
 or water

6 cloves of garlic, peeled

2 x 85g bags of watercress

25g fresh coriander

25g fresh chives

1 tablespoon salt

4 tablespoons vegetable oil

1 large onion, thinly sliced

50g butter

2 tablespoons Bengali spice
 mix (*panch phoran* – see
 p. 237)

2 large red chillies, sliced

240g smoked trout flakes

6 hard-boiled eggs

paprika, to serve

Start by washing the quinoa and setting it aside to drain. Put the stock into a blender with the garlic, watercress, coriander, chives, salt and 2 tablespoons of oil, and blend to a smooth paste.

Heat the other 2 tablespoons of oil in a medium non-stick pan on a high heat. Add the onions and cook, stirring occasionally until they turn a dark brown. As soon as they do, turn the heat down and add the butter and Bengali spice mix – when the spices start to pop, add the quinoa and 1 litre of water and bring to the boil, stirring all the time. Then lower the heat and leave to simmer until all the liquid has evaporated. Take off the heat and stir in the watercress mixture, sliced chillies and smoked trout flakes.

To serve, dish up the kedgeree and serve with the quartered eggs and a sprinkling of paprika. Any leftovers can be cooled and frozen (remove any hard-boiled eggs from these portions as they'll go rubbery when frozen).

We never really ate flatbreads or chapatis when I was growing up, so I didn't know how to make them until my husband expressed a keen interest when we got married and told me his maximum was 14 in one sitting. That is incentive enough to make these delicious flatbreads. They look like parathas but taste like pizza, and they're even better with a garlic and herb dip on the side.

PIZZA PARATHA

For the parathas

600g plain flour, plus extra for dusting

2 teaspoons salt

2 teaspoons sugar

8 tablespoons vegetable oil

280–300ml boiling water

150g butter, melted

For the pizza filling

80g tomato purée

1 tablespoon dried oregano

40g grated hard cheese (the kind you can find in pots to top your pasta with)

1 clove of garlic, grated

For the dip

100g cream cheese

50g yoghurt

1 clove of garlic, grated

a small handful of fresh chives, finely chopped

a squeeze of lemon

a pinch of salt and pepper

Put the flour, salt and sugar into a bowl and stir in the oil. Make a well in the centre and add the boiling water. Using a palette knife, because the water is still very hot, roughly bring the dough together.

Drop the mixture on to a work surface and knead until you have a smooth dough. This should take a few minutes. Pop it into the bowl again and leave to rest, covered.

Meanwhile you can make the filling and dip. To make the filling, put the tomato purée, oregano, cheese and garlic into a bowl and give it a mix. To make the dip, put the cream cheese, yoghurt, garlic, chives, lemon and pepper into another bowl, mix and leave in the fridge.

Roll the dough out into a long sausage shape and cut it into 12 equal portions. Roll each one into a ball and leave them in a pile on the side. Take one ball and roll it out to a circle as thin as you can get it – you should be able to see the work surface through the dough in places.

Take a teaspoon of the tomato mixture, which should be like a paste, and spread it lightly all over the dough. Roll the dough inwards like a Swiss roll, making sure to pinch and stretch it at the ends as you go along. Set aside and repeat with all of the balls of dough.

Take each dough sausage and roll inwards to create what looks like a cinnamon swirl, tucking the end into the base. Melt the butter and have a pastry brush at the ready. Now lightly flour the work surface and roll each paratha out to about a 3mm thin round circle.

Pop a non-stick pan on a medium heat. Place one paratha at a time in the pan and cook gently for 3 minutes on each side. Brush both sides with melted butter and leave on a plate, with a piece of foil over the top to keep them warm while you make the rest. Serve straight away with the dip, as a light lunch.

These parathas are best frozen uncooked, layered with baking parchment in between so they don't stick.

MAKES: 12

TOTAL TIME: 1 HOUR

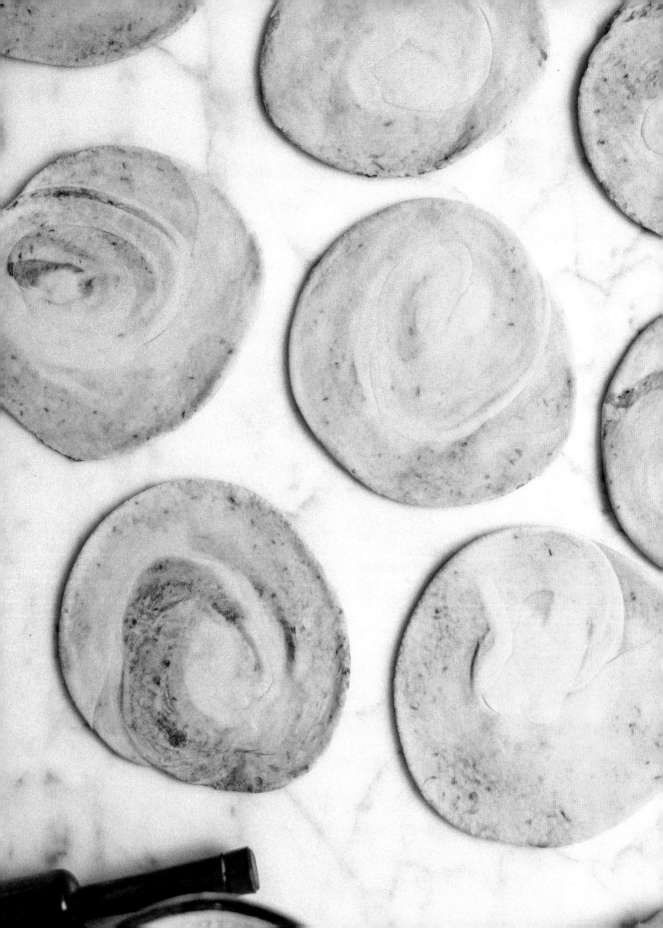

These are delicious cooked and served immediately, but if you have more than you need, they freeze perfectly with a sheet of kitchen paper placed between each paratha. They will freeze for up to 6 months.

DINNER

A good teriyaki is made even more delicious when the fish is left to sit in the sauce overnight in the fridge, but there is nothing to say that it can't be instant. It can, and it should be. We can have delicious food and eat it straight away. Best of all, you can make this, have your dinner and put some fillets into the freezer for another day. And while the fish cooks you can mix up a quick mango salsa to go with it.

TERIYAKI SALMON WITH MANGO SALSA

For the teriyaki salmon

150ml water

1 teaspoon cornflour

4 tablespoons soy sauce

4 tablespoons runny honey

1 tablespoon fish sauce

½ tablespoon ground ginger

½ tablespoon garlic granules

½ tablespoon chilli flakes

4 salmon fillets

250g ready-cooked basmati rice

2 tablespoons vegetable oil, for frying

white sesame seeds (optional)

For the salsa

500g mango chunks or a 420g tin of mango, drained

1 lime, zest and juice

1 tablespoon dried coriander or a small handful of fresh coriander, chopped

1 red chilli, frozen or fresh

Start by making the teriyaki sauce. Put the water into a bowl with the cornflour and stir until the water is cloudy. Now add the soy sauce, honey, fish sauce, ginger, garlic granules and chilli flakes, and stir. Add the salmon fillets and leave them to sit while you make the mango salsa.

Chop the mango into bite-size pieces and put into a bowl. Mix in the zest and juice of the lime and the coriander. If you are using fresh chilli, chop it finely and stir it in, or, if you have some frozen red chillies in the freezer, simply grate one in and mix.

Now cook the rice in the microwave as per the instructions.

Place a non-stick frying pan (ideally one with a lid, but a sheet of foil will do) on a medium to high heat and add the oil. Add 2 salmon fillets, along with half the teriyaki liquid. Leave the rest in the bowl for now.

Cook for 2 minutes on one side, depending on the thickness of the fillet, then flip over and cook for 2 minutes on the other. Make sure that with all the honey in the sauce it isn't sticking or getting too thick – if it is, just turn the heat down and give the sauce a stir. Turn the heat off and cover with a lid or a piece of foil. The trapped heat will steam the thickest part of the fillet.

Before serving, put the remaining liquid and the other 2 fillets into a freezer bag and stick it in the freezer ready for the next time you want teriyaki. Serve up the rice alongside the mango salsa, top with the rest of the salmon, and drizzle over the sauce with a small sprinkling of sesame seeds.

SERVES: 2   TOTAL TIME: 20 MINUTES

Sometimes I want to eat something light and quick, and soup does not have to be laborious or long-winded, and even when you're doing quick and easy you can plan for the week ahead. This recipe uses bits out of jars that, when put together, can make something altogether delicious. And while you're making the soup you can be baking some spicy seeds to go on top and to snack on later.

THAI RED PEPPER SOUP

For the soup

4 tablespoons vegetable oil

3 teaspoons garlic paste

4 teaspoons Thai red curry paste

1 teaspoon salt

1 x 480g jar of roasted red peppers, drained

1.5 litres boiling water

2 slices of bread, stale or fresh, the middle or the thick end

250ml coconut milk

1 tablespoon dried coriander

For the spicy seeds

1 egg white

450g sunflower seeds

½ teaspoon salt

½ teaspoon caster sugar

1 teaspoon paprika

1 teaspoon garlic granules

50g desiccated coconut

1 teaspoon dried coriander

Start by making the soup. This is almost an all-in-one, whack-the-lid-on kind of job, but you will notice I said almost – everything benefits from cooking out, especially the Thai red curry paste.

First, preheat the oven to 180°C/fan 160°C, ready for making the spicy seeds later.

Put the oil into a large saucepan and bring the heat up to medium. Add the garlic paste, red curry paste and salt and cook the paste out. If it starts to stick, turn the heat down and add a splash of water to stop it burning.

Meanwhile, drain the roasted red peppers. Chop them up roughly and add them to the curry paste mixture. Pour in the boiling water – this helps to speed up the process. Tear in chunks of the bread and bring back to the boil, then leave it on a rapid simmer.

Now make your spicy seeds. Whisk the egg white in a bowl until the mixture is foamy. Stir in the sunflower seeds, making sure all of them have an even coating. Sprinkle in the salt, sugar, paprika and garlic granules and mix well, without using your spoon (otherwise all the flavour will stick to it!).

Toss in the desiccated coconut and coriander, then spread the seeds on a baking sheet in an even layer. Bake in the oven for 10–12 minutes, but be sure to keep an eye on them – they will need turning halfway. Once the seeds are dry to touch, they are ready to go. Take them out of the oven and set aside.

Meanwhile add the coconut milk to the pan of soup, stir through, then whiz until smooth, using a stick blender.

To serve, ladle the soup into bowls and sprinkle over some of those delicious spicy sunflower seeds and a drizzle of oil, if you like. There will be plenty of soup to freeze, and the best way to do this is in individual portions. As for the seeds, you will have plenty of those to sprinkle on whatever you like or just for snacking. Store them in a clean jar.

I don't always like having a sit-down dinner. I quite like simple things that can be eaten while watching TV. I'm pretty sure that's the same for most of us. Busy lives sometimes mean quick dinners. This is really easy to make – it's sweet with a hint of spice, and, best of all, I always make plenty to store in the fridge or freezer for another day. It uses tinned cod roe, something I don't think we use often enough.

COD ROE PÂTÉ

3 tablespoons vegetable oil

150g butter (salted or unsalted, whatever you have)

2 medium onions, chopped

1 teaspoon sugar

3 x 200g tins of hard cod roe, cut into small cubes

1 teaspoon chilli powder

2 teaspoons curry powder

1 teaspoon garam masala

150ml double cream

To eat

crispbread or crackers or a plate of toast

aubergine pickle (that's the one I like to eat it with), or a pickle of your choice

This is the simplest thing – at most, all you need is to take some time to cook the onions. Put the oil and butter into a pan and when the butter has melted, add your onions. Cook for 5 minutes on a medium to high heat until the onions are soft, then add the sugar and cook for another 5 minutes. You can also use crisp fried onions. Just omit the oil and use the butter only, on a low heat, as the fried onions already have oil in them and just need warming through.

Once the onions are a deep brown you are good to go. Mix in the cod roe, chilli powder, curry powder and garam masala, then, pressing down with the back of a wooden spoon, cook for another 5 minutes, until the mixture looks bone dry and the spices are well combined.

Put the cod roe mixture into a food processor along with the double cream and blitz until you have a smooth paste. You may need to add another couple of tablespoons of cream to get it really smooth.

The trickiest bit is deciding how much you will eat, how much you will save and what will be frozen. I like to eat my pâté warm with crispbreads and some sweet aubergine pickle. But before tucking in, take the time to decant some into freezer-safe tubs so you have pâté whenever you want – or it can be cooled, kept in the fridge and used as a sandwich spread (bring back to room temperature before serving).

The pâté will keep in the fridge for 3 days. Freeze leftovers in a tub or freezer bag.

SERVES: 4+   TOTAL TIME: 30–40 MINUTES

Anything eaten between two bits of bread is a winner. I always buy these enormous mushrooms and feel sad when I chop them up. They are so big and bold and it seems natural to keep them as they are. So here these massive mushrooms are grilled whole with loads of butter and loaded with mozzarella. Add some brioche and horseradish cream and you don't even need any sides.

MUSHROOM MOZZARELLA BURGER

6 Portobello mushrooms, any long stalks trimmed

125g garlic butter (you can buy this, but to make your own just mix some softened butter with a teaspoon of garlic granules)

salt, to taste

2 large mozzarella balls, sliced into 6 large discs

6 brioche burger buns, halved

6 tablespoons horseradish cream

rocket, to serve

You will need a tray large enough to fit the 12 burger bun halves.

Preheat the grill on the highest setting or preheat the oven to 200°C/fan 180°C. Place the mushrooms on the tray, with the underside facing upwards. This will allow for the butter to be soaked into the little gaps between the gills. Mushrooms are like sponges, and if they are going to soak anything up it should be garlic butter.

Divide the garlic butter between the 6 mushrooms and grill for 5 minutes, until the butter has melted and the mushrooms are slightly shrivelled.

Take off the grill and pop a bun base on top of each mushroom to soak up all that butter. Once the butter has soaked into the bread, remove the bun base and divide the mozzarella slices among the mushrooms. Put the bun base back on and flip over, so that you now have the dome of the mushroom facing upwards.

Put the burger bun tops on the same tray, cut side facing up, and grill for 2 minutes. Watch over them, as the brioche bread can toast very quickly. If you can't fit them all on, toast the tops on a separate tray for 1–2 minutes.

Take off the grill and spread each bun top with some horseradish cream and a small handful of rocket leaves. Pop the top on the base and the buns are ready to eat.

This is a messy eat and loaded with butter, but I wouldn't have it any other way, so enjoy it with a napkin. If you are saving these or have some left over, which I always do, they make great lunches. Wrap them individually in foil and reheat when you need them.

If you are saving some for the week ahead, be sure not to include the rocket leaves, as they wilt and don't taste very good.

If you are making your own garlic butter, double the quantity and keep it in the fridge – it's handy for lots of other dishes.

SERVES: 6   ACTIVE TIME: 10 MINUTES   TOTAL TIME: 15 MINUTES

I never ate sausages until I was about twenty-four. I was always curious, but I could never find any halal sausages, and then, when I did find them, they were always in huge packs of sixteen. So I always cooked more than I needed, even after having a full English. This is a simple cut-corners-type sausage and mash with all the fragrance of Bengali five-spice. I would put the spice in everything if I could, but I won't. However, it does very well in this recipe, when you occasionally bite into a whole spice. We make two here – one for now and one for your freezer.

BENGALI BANGERS AND HASH SMASH

2 x 700g packs of frozen hash browns

2 tablespoons vegetable oil

½ teaspoon Bengali spice mix (*panch phoran* – see p. 237)

16 sausages, cut in half lengthways (I like chicken sausages, but you can use your faves)

320g onion chutney/ marmalade

½ teaspoon chilli powder

1 teaspoon salt

600ml hot water

3 tablespoons gravy granules

6 tablespoons mayonnaise

1 teaspoon chilli flakes

1 tablespoon dried coriander, or a small handful of fresh coriander, finely chopped

100g mature Cheddar cheese, grated

Start by putting the hash browns into a microwave-safe bowl and defrosting them in the microwave for 10 minutes. You may need to do this in two batches.

Heat the oil in a large non-stick pan. When it's hot, add the Bengali five-spice and, as soon as the whole spices start to pop, add the sausages and allow them to cook for about 5 minutes, until they are golden and slightly curled.

Now add the onion chutney, chilli powder and salt and mix through roughly. Stir in the hot water and, as soon as it comes to the boil, add the gravy granules and stir them in. The mixture should start to thicken straight away. Leave to simmer gently for 10 minutes.

Meanwhile put the hash browns into another large non-stick frying pan or a large, deep wok over a medium heat and use a spoon to break them up into small chunks. As the edges start to crisp up a little, stir in the mayonnaise – this will make it creamy and help the spices to stick. Add the chilli flakes and coriander and mix through.

Dinner is ready, but first, put half the sausage mixture into an oven-safe dish (approx. 25cm x 20cm) so you can freeze it for another time. Add just a few spoons of the gravy and top with half the hash brown mixture. Set aside to cool completely before freezing.

Now you can have dinner. Serve sprinkled with the cheese.

To reheat, preheat the oven to 180°C/fan 160°C and bake for 40 minutes from frozen, keeping it covered all the time, except for the last 5 minutes.

The reason why I love this recipe so much is that I always know I will get two for one here. The roast chicken is in a tray and the couscous is cooked in the same one. What I never do is throw the carcass away, because that is full of lovely shreds of meat and juices from the bones and with that I make my chicken soup.

ROAST CHICKEN WITH LEMON COUSCOUS

1 x 1.7kg whole chicken

a drizzle of oil

salt and pepper

5 small red onions, peeled
  and quartered

3 preserved lemons, halved

10 anchovy fillets

250g pearl couscous

500ml boiling water

a large handful of fresh
  parsley, chopped

Heat the oven to 200°C/fan 180°C.

Put the chicken into a roasting dish, drizzle generously with oil, and sprinkle liberally with salt and pepper. Add the onions, preserved lemons and anchovy fillets, then cover with foil and cook for 1 hour 15 minutes.

Take the dish out of the oven and take off the foil, then move the chicken to one side of the tray and bring the ingredients on the base together. Squash the lemons and anchovies with the back of a fork. Stir in the couscous, then pour in the hot water, give it a stir and pop it back into the oven for another 15 minutes, uncovered.

Take out of the oven again and leave for 10 minutes to allow the moisture to absorb into the couscous and the chicken to rest. Stir in the parsley.

Carve the chicken and serve with the couscous.

CHICKEN SOUP

Once dinner is done, collect the carcass and all the bones and pop them into a large pan, along with 1.5 litres of cold water. Peel and quarter 2 medium potatoes (about 500g) and drop those straight in, along with 1 teaspoon of garlic paste, ½ teaspoon of salt and 2 tablespoons of dried tarragon. Bring to the boil, then reduce the heat and cook gently on a medium heat for at least 1 hour with the lid on the pan. The chicken on the carcass should be soft and the potatoes so soft they should be falling apart.

Take the bones out, then take off all the chicken and put it back into the pan. Use the back of a fork to squash the potatoes down a little – this will thicken the soup. This is a good base if you want to add the odd vegetable or two and simmer until they are tender, otherwise it is ready to eat.

If you have any leftovers, this soup freezes really well.

SERVES: 4–6   ACTIVE TIME: 5 MINUTES   TOTAL TIME: 1 HOUR 45 MINUTES

This is something I used to cook for my kids when they were much younger, and I still make it sometimes among the floods of recipes that I test. I don't like spaghetti hoops as they are, neat out of the tin, but I can really appreciate their sweetness and ability to bulk out a dish when they are mixed with other things. So this is exactly that – lots of white fish, mixed with a few vegetable-drawer staples and canned hoops and topped with breadcrumbs. If you're making one of these it's worth making two, as we do here, so that one can sit in your freezer until next time.

HOOP FISH BAKE

2 x 380g pollock fillets, defrosted and chopped into bite-size chunks

10 cherry tomatoes, halved, or 2 tomatoes, chopped

3 spring onions, finely chopped

2 red chillies, thinly sliced

7 florets of broccoli, chopped roughly (or you could use frozen defrosted broccoli, with all the moisture squeezed out)

1 teaspoon salt

1 teaspoon smoked paprika

2 x 385g tins of spaghetti hoops, drained

For the breadcrumb topping

4 small slices of bread or 2 large (approx. 100g)

1 teaspoon garlic granules

½ teaspoon salt

3 tablespoons olive oil

Have two oven- and freezer-safe dishes, approx. 20cm x 26cm, at the ready. I like to use the ones that have plastic lids.

Preheat the oven to 180°C/fan 160°C.

Start by putting the fish into a bowl – if there is too much liquid, squeeze out any extra water by hand so the dish doesn't end up being too wet.

Add the chopped tomatoes, spring onions, chillies and broccoli and mix together. Stir in the salt and paprika, then mix in the drained hoops.

Divide the mixture equally between the two dishes and level the top.

To make the breadcrumb topping, put the bread, garlic granules, salt and oil into a food processor and whiz until you have fine crumbs. Top each dish with half the breadcrumbs and bake for 30 minutes.

Serve one dish as soon as it comes out of the oven, and leave the other one to cool completely, then cover and freeze.

Growing up in Luton, you can't often make chicken and chips as good as the ones that come out of the chicken shop that's open until 3 a.m. But when time is short and with kids looking up at me, I like to try, and God loves a trier. Nothing about this feels like a takeaway, but I love chicken and potatoes any which way. This is how I cook them in the week, but they're great for summer weekend barbecues too.

PIRI DRUMSTICKS, CHIPS AND PEA SALSA

500g frozen oven chips

For the chicken

10 chicken drumsticks, with the skin still on

1 x 45g jar of paprika

1 x 44g jar of chilli powder

1 x 12g jar of dried oregano

1 x 14g jar of ground ginger

1 x 42g jar of garlic granules

1 x 42g jar of onion granules

5 tablespoons salt

4 teaspoons vegetable oil, for roasting

For the pea salsa

375g frozen peas

1 teaspoon ginger paste

1 small red onion, finely chopped

a sprinkling of salt

1 lemon, juice and zest

a handful of fresh coriander

Score the drumsticks, cutting through the skin and just a little bit into the flesh. Pop them into a pan and pour over enough boiling water to cover them completely. Put the pan on the hob and bring to the boil, then reduce the heat and leave to simmer for 10 minutes.

Meanwhile make the peri sprinkle by putting the paprika, chilli powder, oregano, ginger, garlic granules, onion granules and salt into a screwtop jar. Put the lid on and give it a good shake to mix everything together.

Preheat the oven to 220°C/fan 200°C.

Put the oven chips on a baking tray. Drain the drumsticks and put them into a roasting dish. Pat the chicken dry with kitchen paper, then drizzle over the oil and massage it into the chicken when it's cool enough to handle.

Sprinkle the spice mix over the drumsticks, using enough to make a generous coating. Put them into the oven, along with the tray of frozen chips, and bake for 20–25 minutes. Or, if you're doing them on the barbecue, put them on for 10–15 minutes, until cooked through.

Meanwhile, make the pea salsa. Defrost the peas by pouring boiling water over them. This should only take a minute. Drain the peas and put them into a bowl, then, using the back of a fork or a rolling pin, lightly crush them with the ginger paste, chopped onion, salt, lemon juice and zest, and coriander.

By the time the salsa is made, the chicken and chips will be ready to serve. Set aside 4 drumsticks to cool, so they can be frozen in a tub or bag and eaten on another occasion.

We were in Canada not long ago and one of the first things I asked when I went there was, 'What shall we eat?' The same question we always ask ourselves. So many of our breaks are dictated by what we will eat. Canada didn't disappoint. Poutine is a Canadian 'thing', and quite a thing it is too. I love chips and it turns out so do they, but with curd cheese and mushroom gravy. So that's what I'm doing here. Anywhere where they adorn their chips in this way is a place I intend to revisit, but, until then, it happens in my kitchen.

POUTINE

2 tablespoons vegetable oil

2 tablespoons garlic paste

2 mugfuls of frozen onions, or 2 medium onions, chopped

1 tablespoon salt

750g chestnut mushrooms, quartered

1 teaspoon dried rosemary

1 teaspoon dried thyme

1 litre vegetable stock (1 litre boiling water mixed with 4 stock cubes)

1 tablespoon yeast extract

4 tablespoons cornflour

1 tablespoon cocoa powder

700g oven chips

500g halloumi cheese, diced into small 1cm pieces

Begin by making the gravy. I'm making more than I need, as this gravy is great for freezing, so you don't have to make it again when you need it, be it for your poutine or your Sunday roast.

Heat the oil in a large pan, then add the garlic and onions, along with the salt, and cook on a high heat until the onions are soft but a deep golden brown. If it starts to stick, add a splash of water.

Stir in the mushrooms, rosemary and thyme, then add the stock and yeast extract and bring to the boil.

Mix the cornflour and cocoa with 3 tablespoons of water in a bowl, then add to the mushrooms and simmer gently while you cook the chips as per the packet instructions.

Have the halloumi cubes ready to serve. Once the gravy is thick, take it off the heat and use a stick blender to make it smooth. That's the way I remember it, but if you want a chunky version that's okay too.

Serve a heap of chips, sprinkle over the halloumi, and drench in the mushroom gravy.

Whatever gravy you have left, cool and freeze.

SERVES: 4   TOTAL TIME: 50 MINUTES

What I want to do one day is write a book about the versatility of a fish finger. There's something about these perfectly rectangular, golden fishy beauties that I cannot resist. So I have found yet another way to eat them. For all the times you may have thought, 'I only have a box of fish fingers in the freezer,' think of all the things you could have done. Enchiladas for one. We are making two batches with this recipe. One for dinner now, one for later on in the week or month. Just halve the ingredients if you prefer to only make today's.

FISH FINGER ENCHILADA

20 fish fingers, defrosted

2 small red onions, thinly sliced

1 x 326g tin of sweetcorn

100g full-fat cream cheese

1 teaspoon freshly ground black pepper

8 tortilla wraps

500g passata

1 teaspoon salt

1 teaspoon chilli flakes

1 teaspoon garlic granules

1 teaspoon dried basil

200g Cheddar cheese, grated

Preheat the oven to 200°C/fan 180°C, and have two baking dishes at the ready.

Put the defrosted fish fingers into a bowl and crush gently, using the back of a fork. Add the sliced onions, then mix in the corn, cream cheese and black pepper.

Spread the tortillas out and divide the fish mixture between them. Fold and roll so you can get 4 of them into the dish comfortably, then lay those in the dish, seam-side down.

To make the sauce, put the passata into a bowl with the salt, chilli flakes, garlic granules and basil and mix well.

Spoon half the sauce all over the wraps in the dish and sprinkle over half the cheese.

Bake in the oven for 35–40 minutes, until the fish fingers are cooked and the cheese is bubbly. Serve with salad.

Put the other 4 filled wraps into a freezer-safe baking dish, add the rest of the sauce and cheese, then cover the dish with foil and pop into the freezer.

SERVES: 2 HUNGRY,
4 NOT SO HUNGRY

ACTIVE TIME: 10 MINUTES   TOTAL TIME: 50 MINUTES

I love fish, mostly when it is teamed up with citrus, and this is my take on that combination using marmalade, which most of us have knocking about the house. It's fresh and zingy and although it sounds unusual, it tastes good. You can use fresh new potatoes instead if you prefer – they should take the same amount of time to cook as the tinned variety.

MARMALADE HADDOCK

2 x 550g tins of new potatoes, drained and halved

3 sun-dried tomatoes (the antipasti kind, in oil), snipped into strips, plus 1 tablespoon oil from the jar

a drizzle of balsamic vinegar, about 1 tablespoon

a pinch of salt

4 haddock fillets

For the topping

6 tablespoons marmalade

1 teaspoon salt

2 teaspoons garlic paste

2 teaspoons chilli flakes

4 tablespoons dried dill

60g panko breadcrumbs

Preheat the oven to 220°C/fan 200°C.

Put the halved potatoes into a large roasting dish, along with the tomatoes, oil, balsamic and salt, and give it all a really good stir. Place in the oven for 10–15 minutes to warm the potatoes through.

To make the topping, put the marmalade, salt, garlic paste, chilli flakes, dill and breadcrumbs into a food processor and whiz everything together. Take half the mixture and spread it all over the fish. Put the rest of the topping into a freezer bag and freeze, ready for the next time you need breadcrumbs for fish or chicken.

Take the tray of potatoes out of the oven and place the fish on top. Put back into the oven and bake for 15 minutes, until the fish is cooked and the topping is crunchy.

Freeze any leftovers in a tub.

SERVES: 4   ACTIVE TIME: 15 MINUTES   TOTAL TIME: 45 MINUTES

Nut butters are so versatile, especially peanut, and whenever I run out, I just make my own. It's cheaper and so much easier. And it can be used for much more than just breakfast – it's great with chicken and even better when you can have it for dinner. You make enough here to have a jar in your cupboard too.

ONE-TRAY PEANUT CHICKEN

For the peanut butter

500g salted peanuts

1 teaspoon salt (optional – you may find it salty enough with the salted peanuts)

1 tablespoon honey

4–5 tablespoons vegetable oil

For the chicken

250g gnocchi

1kg deboned and skinless chicken thighs, thinly sliced

4 tablespoons honey

4 tablespoons vegetable oil

5 tablespoons Thai green curry paste

5 tablespoons peanut butter (100g)

1 teaspoon salt

2 heads of broccoli, cut into florets

2 small red onions, cut into small wedges

3 tablespoons salted peanuts, roughly chopped

a handful of fresh coriander, roughly chopped

juice of 1 lime

To make the peanut butter, put the nuts into a processor with the salt and honey and blitz till the whole thing starts to change texture. Add the oil slowly and watch as it turns to butter before your very eyes. As soon as it's smooth and shiny, stop and transfer the mixture to a jar.

Preheat the oven to 200°C/fan 180°C and have a roasting dish (about 30cm x 22cm x 5cm) at the ready.

Bring a pan of water to the boil, then add the gnocchi. Boil until they come to the surface, then take off the heat, drain and set aside.

Put the chicken into a large bowl. Add the honey, oil, curry paste, peanut butter and salt, and mix it all well with your hands, massaging in all that flavour. Then put it into the roasting dish along with the broccoli, onions and gnocchi and bake for 30 minutes, giving it a stir halfway through.

Serve topped with the chopped nuts, coriander and a squeeze of lime.

Freeze any leftovers in a tub or freezer bag.

When I was younger, I had only ever seen the word 'dansak' written on Dad's restaurant menus, and I used to watch them sizzling past me on a hot plate. We didn't eat curries like that at home. But now I always enjoy the wholesome thick nature of a dansak – it's hearty, warm and full of flavour. It's great if someone else is making it, but when I'm doing it I want to make it quickly and often in double portions, so that I can enjoy it twice for half the work.

LAMB DANSAK

100g butter

5 tablespoons vegetable oil

2 tablespoons garlic paste

2 tablespoons ginger paste

200g onions, chopped

1 tablespoon salt

2 tablespoons chilli paste

1 tablespoon tomato purée

1 tablespoon curry powder

2 tablespoons garam masala

1 teaspoon ground cinnamon

1kg lamb (neck, shoulder or leg), diced into small cubes

2 tins of kidney beans, drained

To serve

rice

cream

fresh coriander, chopped

Put the butter into a large pan with the oil and let it melt. Then turn up the heat, add the garlic paste, ginger paste, onions and salt, and cook on a high heat until the onions are very brown and soft. Keep a jug of water handy in case they start to stick – if they do, just splash in a little water.

Add the chilli paste, tomato purée, curry powder, garam masala and ground cinnamon, and cook on a medium heat until the mixture really starts to thicken.

Add the lamb and leave to cook till the lamb is browned. Then put a lid on the pan and let it cook gently for 10 minutes.

In the meantime, put the drained kidney beans into a bowl and give them a little squash with the end of a rolling pin to help them break up a little. Dansak is traditionally made with lentils, but lentils take longer, so I use tinned kidney beans instead – plus I love that deep purple colour. Stir the beans into the lamb, pop the lid on again, and cook for 20 minutes over a medium heat.

Cook some rice now, or, if you are still short of time, get a few of those pre-cooked rice packets into the microwave.

I like to serve this with a tiny splash of cream drizzled over, and some chopped coriander. A pineapple salsa also works as a refreshing side – just toss chunks of pineapple with chopped red chillies, red onion and fresh coriander.

Remember, there is enough curry here for two meals, so you can freeze the leftovers.

SERVES: 4　　TOTAL TIME: 50 MINUTES

There's nothing I like more than eating a pasty the size of my head. I've only visited Cornwall a handful of times, but during those times the variations in pasties were shocking. I had a good go at trying as many as possible, learning the basics, the traditions and the out-there flavours. They were filled with everything from chocolate to tikka! Some had butter pastry, others were more bready; some pleased, others depressed. So here I have taken the traditional flavours and kind of changed it around a bit, and changed the way I do it too. Make some now, save some for another day, but I applaud you if you can consume three human-head-sized pasties in one sitting!

SHORTCUT BEEF PASTY

2 small red onions, diced

1 medium potato, grated

2 small parsnips, grated

2 sheets of ready-rolled puff pastry

1 egg, beaten

225g beef mince

4 knobs of butter (about 10g each)

Put the onions into a large bowl. I like using red onions, because they add a tiny bit of colour, not so much once they are cooked but enough to see a slight difference, along with the lovely onion flavour. That onion flavour is one of my favourite parts of the whole pasty.

Traditionally the contents of a pasty would be thinly sliced, but to ensure that everything is cooked all the way through, I am grating the potato and parsnip instead. Take the grated potato and squeeze out any excess liquid, then add to the bowl of onions. Add the grated parsnips – I know these are not traditional, but they still add a lovely sweetness, plus I prefer grating parsnips (swedes are a bit fiddly).

Preheat the oven to 200°C/fan 180°C and have a large oven tray standing by.

Unroll the pastry and cut both sheets across the centre, widthways. Brush the edges of the pastry lightly with a little of the beaten egg.

Give the onion mixture a stir, then divide between the 4 pieces of pastry, piled high on one half, leaving the other half free, as you need to fold it over. Season generously with salt and pepper. Divide the beef mince into four and pile on top of the vegetables. Season well again. Add a knob of butter to each pile of filling.

Carefully fold over the pastry and press to seal the edges, then brush each pasty with more of the beaten egg and sprinkle the top with salt. Cut a slit in the top to allow steam out. Now bake in the oven for 35–40 minutes. Give it a breath before you eat it, as it will be really hot.

My mission in life is to eat every kind of fry, and it would be rude not to share my ideas or my experiences with you. I recently watched a show where they served lava fries in an American diner, and I was like, 'That's it, I'm making those,' and that's what I did. They are spicy and hot and mountain-like, dripping with chilli and soured cream. I don't know if it's authentic, but the slow descent of the sauce down the fries makes them look like an erupting volcano. This is not for the faint-hearted. There's enough here to freeze some for another day.

LAVA FRIES

750g frozen oven chips

For the masala mince

5 tablespoons vegetable oil

10 cloves of garlic, crushed

2 medium onions, finely diced

1 tablespoon salt

1kg beef mince

3 tablespoons chilli paste

2 tablespoons tomato purée

1 tablespoon paprika

1 tablespoon chilli flakes

1 tablespoon ground cumin

1 tablespoon ground coriander

½ a bottle of Worcestershire sauce

2 tins of tomato soup

fresh coriander, chopped

1 can of kidney beans, drained (for the chilli)

For the topping

300ml soured cream

50ml whole milk

2 tablespoons onion granules

1 tablespoons garlic granules

1 teaspoon salt

1 x 210g jar of jalapeños, drained and finely chopped

100g Cheddar cheese, grated

Preheat the oven ready to cook the chips, according to the instructions on the packet. Then start making the masala mince. Put the oil into a large pan on a high heat. Add the garlic, and as soon as it starts to brown, add the onions and salt and cook until the onions are golden and soft.

Add the beef mince and cook until browned, then add the chilli paste, tomato purée, paprika, chilli flakes, cumin, coriander and Worcestershire sauce, and cook for 5 minutes.

Pour in the tomato soup, stir, then leave to simmer on a medium heat until the mixture is very thick, stirring occasionally.

Now pop the chips into the preheated oven and cook as instructed.

Make the topping by mixing the soured cream with the milk, onion granules, garlic granules and salt.

To finish the masala mince, stir in the coriander. Divide the mince mixture in half and mix in the kidney beans to make a chilli for another day.

Once the chips are done, pile them up in an oven-safe serving dish. Pile the mince on top of them, sprinkle over the jalapeños, then scatter over the cheese and grill on high until the top is toasted.

Allow leftover mince to cool, then freeze in a tub or bag. You could serve it another day with rice and soured cream, sprinkled with fresh coriander and chopped chillies.

I like the idea of having an alternative to chicken, and for us, a leg of lamb is a real treat. A butterflied leg of lamb is basically a leg of lamb with the bone taken out, which makes it easier to cook and easier to carve as there's no bone to cut around. Perfect for the oven and even better on the barbecue. Cooked simply, it's finished with a fragrant rhubarb and rosemary glaze.

BUTTERFLIED LAMB LEG WITH A RHUBARB AND ROSEMARY GLAZE

whole leg of lamb, butterflied (you can get your butcher to do this, or buy it already done)

oil, for coating

2 tablespoons salt

For the rhubarb glaze

50g butter

2 large sprigs of rosemary, leaves removed from stalks and finely chopped

4 cloves of garlic, chopped

400g rhubarb, thinly sliced

½ teaspoon salt

2 tablespoons honey

1 teaspoon chilli powder

Start by preheating the oven to 180°C/fan 160°C. If the leg of lamb is thicker in places, lay it on a board and make vertical slices, then open it up. This will help it to cook evenly.

Pop into a large roasting dish.

Drizzle over the oil and be generous. Cover both sides. Sprinkle over the salt and, again, don't be afraid to be generous – that's a big bit of meat and it needs seasoning well.

Pop it into the oven for 40 minutes if you like the meat medium, or 30 minutes if you prefer it pink. While it's cooking, make the glaze.

Melt the butter in a pan. Next add the rosemary and garlic and cook them on a high heat for just a few minutes. Lower the heat to medium and add the rhubarb, salt, honey and chilli powder, then stir.

Increase the heat slightly and mix occasionally. As it cooks it should resemble lava bubbling. You need to cook this for about 30-40 minutes until you have a rich, deep paste. If it starts to stick, just lower the heat and stir frequently. If you have a particularly tart batch of rhubarb you may like to add an extra 1-2 tablespoons of honey.

Once the leg of lamb has been in the oven for the required cooking time, remove it. If there is any liquid in the base of the roasting dish, carefully drain it off.

Brush the glaze all over the top and base of the meat, and leave it fat-side up to finish cooking.

Once it has cooked for a further 20 minutes, take it out and leave to rest for at least 15 minutes before eating.

TO BARBECUE

Alternatively, you can barbecue the butterflied lamb – it's always good to have options. Once the coals are hot enough, put the seasoned and oiled lamb on to the barbecue, fat-side down, and cook on a high heat for 5 minutes until well browned. Turn over and cook on the other side for 5 minutes to brown the other side too.

Now move the coals from the centre to around the edges of the barbecue and leave the meat to cook, covered, for 30–40 minutes, turning occasionally if you need to.

Take the lamb off the barbecue, cover it with foil and leave to rest for 15 minutes, undisturbed. By which time it is ready to slice and eat.

Sometimes we like to go meat-free during the week, and that's when mushrooms are my saving grace. They are deep in colour and rich in flavour – they give off the aura of meat, but they are not. That's why we love them, and it means we can have a meat-free lasagne too. This is the kind of thing you want to leave on the slow cooker just before popping out, knowing you will have dinner ready for when you get back and another one ready to go in the freezer (if you only want to make one, halve all of the ingredients).

SLOW COOKER MUSHROOM LASAGNE

8 tablespoons vegetable oil

8 cloves of garlic, crushed

2 medium onions, diced

2 teaspoons salt

2 heaped teaspoons cumin seeds

2 x 625g packs of chestnut mushrooms, roughly sliced, or 4 x 285g tins of mushrooms

4 teaspoons freshly ground black pepper

500g mascarpone cream

200ml milk

400g Cheddar cheese, grated

cooking oil spray

12 lasagne sheets

Put the oil into a medium pan on a high heat and as soon as it is hot, add the garlic. When it's golden, add the onions and salt and cook until soft.

Add the cumin seeds, then add the mushrooms and keep cooking on high until they have really reduced in size. Stir in the black pepper and cook until most of the moisture has evaporated, then take off the heat.

To make the easy white sauce, mix together the mascarpone, milk and cheese.

Lightly spray some oil on the inside of your slow cooker pot, and have a medium lasagne dish at the ready.

Put a quarter of the mushroom mixture into the slow cooker, and the other quarter into the lasagne dish, then make a layer of 3 sheets of lasagne in each, breaking the pasta up where necessary to fit.

Layer on a quarter of the mascarpone sauce in the slow cooker, and another quarter in the lasagne dish, followed by the rest of the mushroom mixture and the remaining lasagne sheets, half in each. Finally, spread the rest of the mascarpone mixture on top. Set the lasagne dish aside to cool. Leave the slow cooker on a low setting for 2 hours.

I like to serve this with with garlic bread (see p. 242) and salad.

When the lasagne in the dish has cooled, cover with foil and freeze.

From my travels through Thailand this is a recipe that has stayed with me – it's fragrant, creamy and spicy, warming and delicious. I don't know whose grandmother started this, but whoever she is, we are thankful, because it is one of the best things ever to pass my lips. The paste is pretty versatile – see opposite for other ways you can use it.

GRANDMAMA'S CURRY

For the paste

150g desiccated coconut

50g peppercorns

3 whole bulbs of garlic, peeled

250g ginger, peeled and chopped

120g fresh red chillies, roughly chopped

9 sticks of lemongrass

5 teaspoons ground turmeric

4 tablespoons salt

300ml vegetable oil (you may need more)

To cook

100g desiccated coconut

4 tablespoons paste (see above) per 500ml water

2 tablespoons garlic paste

2 tablespoons ginger paste

250ml coconut cream

about 1.5 litres water

1 whole chicken, skin removed

2 tablespoons cornflour

200g mangetout

200g baby corn, halved lengthways

To serve

rice

a large handful of fresh coriander, chopped

limes, cut into quarters

Start by making the paste. Toast 150g of desiccated coconut until very brown. Put into a blender with the peppercorns, and blend until the peppercorns are broken down. Add the garlic, ginger, chillies, lemongrass, turmeric, salt and oil. Blend till you have a smooth paste. If it isn't moving, scrape the sides down and add some more oil until it does.

Transfer the paste to a large jar. This makes a large amount, and it will keep in the fridge for 6 months.

Put 100g of desiccated coconut into a large pan and toast until dark brown. Take off the heat and stir in the paste, then add the garlic paste, ginger paste and the coconut cream and mix really well.

Add the whole chicken to the pan and pour over the water – you need enough to come about three-quarters of the way up the chicken. Bring to the boil, then reduce the heat and leave the whole thing to cook gently for 1 hour.

Take off the heat and use a slotted spoon to remove the chicken, gently, as it will be falling apart. Place it on a large plate or a board. While the chicken is cooling slightly, turn up the heat under the liquid in the pan and boil rapidly for 10–15 minutes.

Pull the chicken off the bones, using two forks as it will be hot, and get rid of the bones. Put the chicken back into the pan and cook slowly for another 30 minutes with the lid off.

Meanwhile cook enough rice for 6 people.

Mix the cornflour with 3 tablespoons of water in a small bowl, then stir it into the sauce for the last 5 minutes of cooking, together with the mangetout and baby corn.

Put the rice on a platter and pour all the chicken on top. Sprinkle with chopped coriander and serve with wedges of lime.

Leftovers can be frozen in a tub or freezer bag.

SERVES: 6   ACTIVE TIME: 50 MINUTES   TOTAL TIME: 2 HOURS 30 MINUTES

GRANDMAMA'S CURRY PASTE

Once you have a curry paste made up, the possibilities are practically endless. This paste is really versatile. It is a great base for any curry – be adventurous with the protein you choose – use fish, lamb or chunks of good hearty vegetables. It's also great added to instant noodles for extra flavour, and can simply be drunk as a flavoured broth by stirring a teaspoon of the paste into a mug of boiling water.

These do take a little effort to make, and they can get demolished in seconds, but most of the effort is in waiting around. Lots of waiting. But it's worth it – these buns are soft and light, and with the spicy raw tuna it is quite literally a melt-in-the-mouth experience.

BAO BUNS WITH SPICY TUNA

For the buns

500g plain flour

2 teaspoons salt

2 tablespoons sugar

2 teaspoons fast-action yeast

300ml warm water

For the spicy tuna

440g tuna steaks (sashimi grade), finely chopped

2 spring onions, finely chopped

1 red chilli, finely diced, with seeds

2.5cm piece of ginger, peeled and grated

2 tablespoons honey

5 tablespoons soy sauce

2 teaspoons sesame oil

1 tablespoon black or white sesame seeds

a small handful of fresh coriander, chopped

Put the flour, salt, sugar and yeast into a bowl and mix together. Make a well in the centre and add the water, then bring the dough together. If you're using a mixer, knead for 5 minutes on a high speed, and if you're doing it by hand, knead for 10 minutes. The dough should be lovely and shiny and stretchy. Place back in the bowl and leave to prove for 1 hour, covered, in a warm place until doubled in size.

Meanwhile cut out 10 squares of baking parchment measuring 10cm x 10cm and have two baking trays at the ready.

Roll the dough into a sausage shape and cut it into 10 equal pieces (80g each). Roll each one out to a circle 5mm in thickness and brush all over with oil. Brush a chopstick with oil too, then lay it in the centre, fold over the dough to create a semicircle and pull the stick out. Place on a piece of paper and then on a baking tray. Do this to all 10 pieces of dough, then cover with a piece of greased clingfilm and leave for 30 minutes, until doubled in size.

Depending on the size of your steamer, steam as many buns as you can at a time without overcrowding it. They should take 5–6 minutes, until springy to touch.

While the buns are steaming, make the spicy tuna. Put the chopped tuna into a bowl and add the onions, chilli, ginger, honey, soy sauce, sesame oil, sesame seeds and chopped coriander. Snap open the steamed buns and fill them with the spicy tuna.

HANDY TIP

Any leftover tuna mix can be saved in the fridge for the next day, to have with rice, a stir-fry or in a poke bowl, and any leftover buns can be frozen.

MAKES: 6

ACTIVE TIME: 45 MINUTES   TOTAL TIME: 2 HOURS 15 MINUTES

Jackfruit is all the rage at the moment, which is bizarre, because I have been eating the stuff my whole entire life and never batted an eyelid. I like it ripe on my toast, sweet and fragrant. But when still green and not sweet, it makes a great alternative to meat – with its stringy body and firm texture I kind of get it, and it is delicious in a curry.

JACKFRUIT CURRY WITH NO-YEAST NAAN

For the curry

10 cloves of garlic

a 3cm piece of ginger, peeled and chopped

1 medium onion

1 tablespoon salt

100ml vegetable oil

1 teaspoon ground cinnamon

1 teaspoon chilli paste

1 tablespoon tomato purée

1 teaspoon ground turmeric

1 tablespoon curry powder

2 x 565g tins of jackfruit in brine

200ml water

fresh coriander, chopped

½ a lime

For the naan

500g plain flour

2 tablespoons nigella seeds

5 tablespoons sugar

1 teaspoon salt

1 teaspoon baking powder

250ml whole milk

vegetable oil, for brushing

In a food processor, blitz the garlic, ginger, onion and salt to a smooth paste. Add water if you need to, but very little.

Put the oil into a large non-stick pan over a medium heat. Add the cinnamon and fry for 20 seconds. Then add the paste from the processor and cook for 5 minutes – if it starts to stick, add splashes of water. Stir in the chilli paste, tomato purée, turmeric and curry powder.

While that cooks on a medium heat, drain the jackfruit and cut it into small, bite-size pieces. Add them to the pan, then stir in the water and leave to simmer gently until totally dry.

Now start on the naan. Mix the flour in a bowl with the nigella seeds, sugar, salt and baking powder. Make a well in the centre and add the milk, then use a palette knife to bring the dough together. Knead on a floured surface for 10 minutes, or, if you are using a dough hook on a mixer, knead for 5 minutes. Then leave the dough in the bowl for 10 minutes.

Preheat the oven to 240°C/fan 220°C, and put a large baking tray in to get hot.

Divide the dough into 8 equal portions, then roll them all out as thin as you can get them. Take the hot tray out of the oven and brush its surface with oil. Add as many bits of rolled dough as will fit. Bake for 2 minutes, until lightly browned, and lightly brush the tops with oil once you have taken them out of the oven. Repeat until all the dough is cooked.

To finish the jackfruit curry, stir in the coriander, drizzle with a squeeze of fresh lime, and you are ready to eat. There is enough here for 4 meals, so if you have any curry left over, you can freeze it for another day.

You can also freeze any leftover naan breads, or keep them for the next day to make Harissa Bean Pizza (see p. 22).

SERVES: 4   TOTAL TIME: 1 HOUR 10 MINUTES

Paneer is a kind of cheese that is creamy, but meaty enough to withstand being rustled about and cooked furiously. So rather than using mince, I use blitzed paneer to make these cheesy koftas, dipped in an easy sauce, and served with hot vermicelli rice.

PANEER KOFTA WITH VERMICELLI RICE

For the koftas

1 x 226g pack of paneer

1 teaspoon salt

1 teaspoon cumin seeds

1 teaspoon chilli flakes

3 cloves of garlic

1 small onion, roughly chopped

1 medium egg

1 x 400g tin of chickpeas, drained

8 tablespoons chickpea flour

500ml vegetable oil, for frying

For the vermicelli rice

100g vermicelli

1 cinnamon stick

5 bay leaves

150g butter

400g basmati rice, washed and drained

1 teaspoon salt

1 litre boiling water

Begin by making the koftas. Put the paneer chunks into a food processor and whiz until they look minced. Now add the salt, cumin seeds, chilli flakes, garlic, onion, egg and chickpeas and keep whizzing until you can see that the chickpeas have broken down. Now add the chickpea flour and whiz until you have a very thick paste.

Put the oil into a small pan, making sure it comes halfway up. Have a baking tray ready, lined with kitchen paper. Heat the oil on a high heat, then reduce to medium.

Drop heaped teaspoons of the kofta mixture into the oil and fry for 3–4 minutes, making sure to turn them occasionally. Do this till you have finished them all. You should have enough koftas for half to be eaten for dinner now and the other half to be frozen, so set half of them aside to cool.

For the rice, put the vermicelli, cinnamon and bay leaves into a dry pan and turn the heat up to medium. Toast the noodles for a few minutes, until they are a very golden brown. Add the butter and leave it to melt.

Now add the washed rice, along with the salt, and cook for 2 minutes. Pour in the boiling water. Be very careful at this point, as it will hiss and spit when you pour it in. Keep stirring until it comes to the boil, and as soon as it does, keep on stirring until all the water evaporates. Lower the heat, pop a lid on the pan, and leave to steam for 15 minutes.

In the meantime make the sauce by mixing together the yoghurt, tahini, garlic, ginger, maple syrup, curry powder, salt, lime juice and zest in a bowl.

For the sauce

250g Greek yoghurt

150g tahini

2 cloves of garlic, crushed

2.5cm piece of ginger, peeled and grated

1 tablespoon maple syrup

1 tablespoon curry powder

1 teaspoon salt

1 lime, juice and zest

To serve

limes, cut into wedges

When the rice is cooked, serve it with the koftas, with the yoghurt sauce alongside and wedges of lime.

This goes brilliantly with a simple tomato salad, and some fresh coriander.

Both the koftas and the rice can be frozen. Perfect as a sandwich filler or a nibble with a dip if you're having guests over or need a snack in front of the telly that isn't a bag of crisps for a change.

If you have any sauce left, you can loosen it with some olive oil and use it as a salad dressing.

I was raised on fish curry, so brothy, flavourful fish is right up my alley. This is warm and delicious and perfect to dippy-dip with homemade garlic bread. You can double batch the stew, if you like, so you have one in the freezer for another time. Simply double the stew ingredients.

CHORIZO FISH STEW WITH GARLIC BREAD

For the garlic bread

450g plain flour

7g fast-action yeast

1 teaspoon sugar

1 teaspoon salt

50g butter

300ml warm water

2 tablespoons coarse semolina

75g butter, melted

5 cloves of garlic, grated

a small handful of fresh parsley, chopped

a good pinch of rock salt

For the stew

5 tablespoons vegetable oil

230g chorizo, chopped into chunks

2 tablespoons crushed mustard seeds

5 cloves of garlic, crushed

6 tomatoes, peeled and chopped

1 teaspoon salt

1 teaspoon tomato purée

1 teaspoon chilli powder

5 tablespoons malt vinegar

540g white fish chunks (I like to use pollock or basa)

450ml water

120g smoked salmon trimmings

a large handful of fresh parsley, chopped

Start by making the garlic bread. Put the flour, yeast, sugar and salt into a bowl. Add the butter and rub it in. Make a well in the centre and add the water, then bring the dough together and knead for 10 minutes, until it is smooth and stretchy. Put it back into the bowl, cover and leave to prove for 1 hour, or until the dough has doubled in size.

Have ready a roasting tray, lightly greased and with semolina sprinkled over the base. Knock the dough back in the bowl, then tip out on to a floured surface. Divide it into golfball-size pieces and put them on the tray, leaving small gaps in between to give the dough room to grow. Cover and leave to prove until doubled in size.

Now on to the stew. Put the oil into a pan over a medium heat, and when it's hot add the chorizo and cook until some of the spices have been released. Add the mustard seeds and allow them to sizzle. Then add the garlic and cook until golden. Add the chopped tomatoes, salt, tomato purée, chilli powder and vinegar, and cook on a medium heat for 10 minutes.

Preheat the oven to 160°C/fan 140°C and bake the garlic bread for 30–35 minutes.

Now add your white fish to the stew and cook for a few minutes with the lid on. Then take off the lid, add the water and leave to simmer on the lowest heat.

Take the stew off the heat and mix in the salmon and parsley. Put the lid on the pan to keep it hot.

Meanwhile melt the butter and add the garlic, parsley and rock salt. As soon the rolls come out of the oven, brush all the butter on top of the hot rolls.

Serve the stew with the hot garlicky bread.

SERVES: 4

ACTIVE TIME: 1 HOUR
TOTAL TIME: 2 HOURS 30 MINUTES

I ate these momos with cabbage on a mountain in Nepal a while ago and I loved them so much that before I could finish my food it was whisked away. I have the flavour and memory of this beautiful dish etched in my mind and have desperately tried to recreate its magic. I hope I have done it justice. We make a double batch of the soya cabbage here, so you have a meal for another day. It tastes good with rice, as a filling for samosas or toasties, or cold from the fridge on a pasta salad.

TING MOMO WITH SOYA CABBAGE

For the ting momo

250g plain flour, plus a little extra for dusting

1 teaspoon salt

1 tablespoon sugar

1 teaspoon fast-action yeast

150ml warm water

vegetable oil, for greasing

For the soya cabbage

150ml vegetable oil

2 teaspoons mustard seeds

2 teaspoons cumin seeds

2 teaspoons coriander seeds

3 teaspoons chilli flakes

2 medium onions, finely diced

1 large bulb of garlic, peeled and crushed

2 teaspoons salt

2 red peppers, finely diced

1 white cabbage, finely shredded

600g soya mince (or any vegetarian mince of your choice)

1 teaspoon ground turmeric

a large handful of fresh coriander, finely chopped

Start by making the momo dough. Mix together the flour, salt, sugar and yeast in a bowl. Make a well in the centre and add the water, then bring the dough together. Knead for 10 minutes, until smooth, then rub the outside of the dough with a little oil. Grease the inside of a bowl with oil and put in the dough, then cover with clingfilm or a tea towel and leave to rise for an hour, or until it has doubled in size.

Meanwhile, cook the cabbage. Put the oil into a large pan on a medium to high heat. Add the mustard seeds, cumin seeds and coriander seeds, and as soon as they start to pop, add the chilli flakes and give it a quick stir.

Add the onions and turn the heat up to high. Let the onions cook, tossing them around in the oil and spices, until they are golden brown, stirring now and again. Turn the heat down to medium, then add the garlic and salt and cook for a few more minutes.

Add the red peppers and the shredded cabbage and give it all a stir, then add a small splash of water and put the lid on the pan. Reduce the heat to low and leave to steam for 30 minutes, allowing the cabbage to wilt.

Take the dough out of the bowl and put it on a very lightly floured surface. Oil your hands lightly, and oil a steamer generously all over. Flatten the dough and roll it out into a rectangle roughly 40cm x 45cm.

Oil the top layer of the dough lightly all over by hand. With the longest side closest to you, fold one third of the dough over the next third. Take the other third and fold it over the other two. You should have one long rectangle with three layers. Cut it into 4 equal pieces – you should have 4 rectangles.

continued over page ⇥

Take each rectangle and cut it into 6 equal strips. You should treat 6 strips as one ting momo now. Separate them out into 6 individual sections. Place 3 strips on the other 3 strips. Do the same with the rest. You should end up with 4 piles of stacked strips.

Hold the strips at the ends and pinch together, all the time pulling and stretching gently. Give them a twist a few times and twirl as if you were wringing out a towel by the ends. Now twist the whole thing in your hands to create a neat swirl. Tuck in the ends at the bottom and pop into the steamer. Do the same with the other 3 piles of strips and leave to prove for 30 minutes, covered, in a warm place.

Give the cabbage a stir – it should have wilted significantly by now. Add the turmeric and the soya mince, give it all another stir, and leave to cook for a bit longer while the momos are proving. The cabbage lends itself to long, slow cooking – the longer you cook cabbage the tastier it gets – so just leave it on a low heat with a lid on the pan.

When the momos have doubled in size, bring the water under the steamer to the boil. Pop in the momos and steam for 12 minutes – no longer.

Dish up and eat while still warm. The cabbage should be lovely and soft, and because of the long cooking it will have bits that have caught and fried a little more than the rest – those are the best bits.

To eat, take a momo, peel away long pieces and use them to pick up the cabbage.

This is a double batch, so one half of the cabbage needs to be cooled completely. Once cool, put it into a bag and freeze.

finished photo over page ➺

Shawarmas are like the kebabs that you can justify as being good for you. Well, they're not particularly bad for you really, and they are actually quite easy to make. You don't need a roly thing, or a special bread knife or tray. Let me show you how.

CHICKEN SHAWARMA

For the shawarma

2 tablespoons cornflour

1 tablespoon salt

1 teaspoon ground cumin

1 teaspoon dried coriander

1 teaspoon paprika

1 teaspoon ground turmeric

½ teaspoon ground cloves

1 tablespoon cayenne

1 teaspoon ground cinnamon

2 tablespoons vegetable oil

750g boneless chicken
  thighs, halved

For the raw slaw

1 large broccoli floret,
  thinly sliced

300ml Greek yoghurt

4 tablespoons vegetable oil

1 teaspoon mustard powder

1 tablespoon mustard seeds

1 teaspoon salt

fresh parsley, finely chopped

To serve

flatbreads

Preheat the oven to 180°C/fan 160°C and lightly grease a 900g loaf tin.

For the shawarma, mix together the cornflour, salt, cumin, coriander, paprika, turmeric, cloves, cayenne and cinnamon.

Put the oil into a bowl, then add the chicken and stir it around. Add the dry spice mix and stir to coat all the chicken pieces well. Layer the pieces of chicken in the loaf tin and press down, then bake in the oven for 40 minutes.

Meanwhile, make the slaw. Put the broccoli into a large bowl.

Put the yoghurt into a second bowl and heat the oil in a small pan. As soon as the oil is hot, add the mustard powder and seeds – when the seeds begin to pop, pour the oil and seeds over the yoghurt, add the salt and stir. Pour this dressing over the broccoli, then mix in the parsley.

When the shawarma is ready, leave it in the tin for 10 minutes so that all the juices can go back into the chicken.

Tip it out of the tin and slice your shawarma. We like to eat this piled into flatbreads with the slaw. Any leftovers can be kept in the fridge, or frozen for the next time you need your shawarma fix.

SERVES: 4　　　　ACTIVE TIME: 20 MINUTES　TOTAL TIME: 1 HOUR

I never understood what was meant by tandoori chicken, until I realized it was the type of oven – a tandoor – they were talking about. So I have made the same dish my dad used to serve up in his restaurant, but using our oven at home. It has a similar red hue, but not so red that you'll question whether you will ever sleep again! It's served with an onion salad and burnt butter rice.

'TANDOORI' OVEN CHICKEN WITH BURNT BUTTER RICE

For the chicken

4 skinless chicken thighs and 4 skinless breasts, flesh slashed

2 tablespoons ghee, melted

4 tablespoons tandoori spice mix (see p. 238)

For the sauce

400g yoghurt

5 tablespoons chickpea flour

35g melted ghee

4 tablespoons tomato purée

3 tablespoons tandoori spice mix (see p. 238)

For the rice

500g basmati rice, washed and drained

200g butter

1 teaspoon salt

1 litre boiling water

For the red onion apple salad

2 red onions, thinly sliced

2 green apples, cut into thin sticks

a squeeze of lemon juice

1 teaspoon salt

a small handful of fresh mint

To serve

sliced red chillies, to taste

fresh coriander, chopped

Preheat the oven to 220°C/fan 200°C and have a roasting dish ready that all the chicken will fit into.

Put the chicken into the tray. Massage the ghee into the skin and sprinkle over the tandoori spice mix. Then bake in the oven for 15 minutes.

To make the sauce, put the yoghurt, chickpea flour, ghee, tomato purée and tandoori spice mix into a bowl and combine.

Reduce the oven temperature to 200°C/fan 180°C. Take the chicken out of the oven and pour the yoghurt mix all over the top, then put back into the oven for 30 minutes.

Meanwhile, cook the rice. Put the butter into a large pan on a high heat until it becomes a golden-brown colour. As soon as it does, add the rice and salt and stir. Add the hot water and keep stirring until it comes to the boil – when it does, keep stirring until all the liquid has evaporated. Pop the lid on the pan and leave the rice to steam on a low heat for 10 minutes.

To make the salad, mix together the onions, apples, lemon juice, salt and mint.

When the chicken is ready, sprinkle with red chillies and coriander and serve with the burnt butter rice.

This squash is cooked whole, with slits cut into it so all the flavour can permeate through. It's served with a simple burnt garlic rice. Sometimes all we want is something hearty with veg, and that is exactly what this is.

HASSELBACK SQUASH WITH BURNT GARLIC RICE

For the squash

1 medium butternut squash

5 tablespoons vegetable oil

1 teaspoon salt

1 tablespoon ginger paste

1 teaspoon chilli flakes

1 tablespoon dried rosemary

1 tablespoon ground cumin

1 lemon, zest and juice

fresh parsley, chopped,
  to finish

For the rice

50ml vegetable oil

100g unsalted butter

1 whole bulb of garlic,
  peeled and sliced

500g basmati rice

1 tablespoon salt

Preheat the oven to 200°C/fan 180°C and have a roasting tray at the ready.

Peel your squash, then take off the top and bottom ends, cut it in half lengthways and scoop out the seedy bits. Now, with the cut side of the squash flat against the chopping board, make slits across it horizontally. Start at the top, working your way down and leaving 5mm gaps, ensuring each slit does not go all the way through the squash. Cut each half all the way through lengthways, so you have 4 individual quarters. Don't worry if you accidentally cut too far when making the slits – just slide the pieces together when you put them on the roasting tray.

Put the oil, salt, ginger paste, chilli flakes, rosemary, cumin, and zest and juice of a lemon, into a bowl and mix together really well.

Put the squash on the roasting tray and smother it with the dressing. Bake in the oven for 30 minutes, until the squash is tender.

Now cook the rice. Put the oil and butter into a large pan over a medium heat. When the butter has melted, add the garlic and cook on a high heat until it is almost black, stirring occasionally. As soon as it is very dark, take the pan off the heat and stir in the rice and salt.

Have a kettle of boiling water ready by your side. Cook the rice on a medium heat for 3 minutes, or until the grains are an opaque white, stirring all the time. Pour in water until it is 1cm above the level of the rice.

Cook the rice on a high heat until all the water has been absorbed, stirring to make sure the rice doesn't stick to the base of the pan. Then turn the heat right down to the lowest setting, pop the lid on, and let the rice steam for 15 minutes.

Serve everyone some squash and rice, and sprinkle over the fresh parsley. You might like to add some Avocado Pesto (p. 27) to this, or the dressing from the Sweet Potato and Goat's Cheese Tart (p. 110).

Any leftover rice can be frozen.

DESSERTS

This doesn't have to be made ahead, as it's so easy to whip together, but if you have any left over, just pop it into the freezer for another time. It's so simple it can be made with any fruit, but I like this combination, not to mention the beautiful colour with flecks of minty green.

MANGO AND PEACH MINT SORBET

500g frozen mango pieces

1 x 411g tin of peaches, drained

4 tablespoons Greek yoghurt

4 tablespoons golden syrup

a small handful of fresh mint, chopped

Pop all the ingredients into a food processor and blitz until it comes together into a thick sorbet-type paste, making sure to occasionally scrape down the sides. If you find the mixture is not moving at any point, add an extra spoon of yoghurt.

While blitzing, you may find it becoming less frozen and more like a smoothie. If this is the case, pop it into the freezer for about 20 minutes before serving.

Store any leftovers in a Tupperware container, placed inside a ziplock bag to keep the sorbet soft and easy to scoop.

MANGO AND PEACH SORBET FLOAT

You can serve any leftover sorbet as a drink: take a scoop of it and put it into the bottom of a glass. Add a few frozen berries if you have any in the freezer, then pour in some lemonade to make the perfect chilled tropical-flavoured drink.

SERVES: 4   TOTAL TIME: 15 MINUTES

This is the simplest mousse, and we all need a quick mousse recipe for when we want dessert or something sweet. I for one love chocolate hazelnut spread, but I also love the spreads that used to be just chocolate bars and have been reborn as the same thing in jars in a spreadable form. You can use whichever you like.

CHOCOLATE HAZELNUT MOUSSE

200g chocolate hazelnut spread

50ml whole milk

600ml double cream

1 tablespoon cornflour

3 tablespoons icing sugar

100g roasted chopped hazelnuts

whippy cream, from a can, to serve (optional)

cocoa powder for dusting, if you feel like it

Pop the chocolate hazelnut spread into a bowl with the milk and heat in the microwave in 10-second bursts until the mixture is runny and viscous, but not steaming hot. This should not take more than 20 seconds. Set aside to cool.

Put the cream into a large bowl with the cornflour and icing sugar and begin whipping. As soon as it begins to thicken, pour in the chocolate mixture and keep whipping until you have stiff peaks.

Fold through the hazelnuts (keeping a tablespoon back for decorating), then spoon into a serving dish or individual ramekins. If you want it to look extra special, you can pipe the mousse in.

Serve with whippy cream if desired, with an extra sprinkling of hazelnuts on top and a dusting of cocoa powder.

MAKES: 1 LARGE DISH OR
8 SMALL RAMEKINS

TOTAL TIME: 20 MINUTES

Does this even need an intro? S'mores are American madness in its best form: crunchy biscuit, melted chocolate and gooey marshmallow. They are not the easiest things to find here, so we often make them for the barbecue over the summer, but when we want a quick dessert this is the best thing ever! All made in a frying pan, with biscuits to dive in.

FRYING PAN S'MORES

300g dark chocolate, chips
    or cut into cubes, or choc
    of your choice

1 x 220g jar of salted caramel

40–45 medium
    marshmallows

400g pack of digestives
    or oat biscuits

For this you will need a frying pan or skillet that is safe to go into the oven, or alternatively you can use a 23cm round cake tin. I use either/or, whatever I have to hand.

Preheat the oven to 200°C/fan 180°C and have the biscuits ready. You want to eat these while they are still hot and oozy, so be prepared.

Layer the base with the cubes of chocolate, or chips if those are what you are using. Spread the caramel all over the top. This is not traditional, it's just an extra element I enjoy.

Carefully place the marshmallows on top, upright, and pack them in tightly. If you don't want to cook this straight away, it will be fine in the fridge until you're ready. Otherwise, bake in the oven for about 7 minutes.

It's ready when the marshmallows are a golden brown and start to puff up.

Time to dig in – take a biscuit and dip it right into the base until you have melted chocolate, runny caramel and stringy marshmallow on your crisp biscuit.

SERVES: 6–8   ACTIVE TIME: 5 MINUTES   TOTAL TIME: 15 MINUTES

Barfi is a delicious Indian sweet traditionally made with condensed milk and milk powder. It is my Abdal's absolute favourite. His eyes light up whenever someone opens up a box in front of him, but they take time and a little more effort to make your own, so this is my easy version. Everything goes into a processor and is blitzed, so if you are taking the appliance out of the cupboard, it's worth making double the amount. I like to eat them out of the fridge as little balls of energy, just perfect for when I need a sweet hit.

COCONUT BARFI TRUFFLES

50g pistachios

150g dried apricots

5 cardamom pods, seeds removed and crushed, or 1 teaspoon ground cardamom

160g desiccated coconut, plus 20g extra for coating

1 orange, zest only

up to 10 tablespoons condensed milk

Put the pistachios into the processor and blitz to crumbs. Add the apricots and blitz until they start falling apart.

Add the cardamom, coconut and orange zest and blitz again to mix everything together.

Now slowly add the condensed milk – this is best done with the kind that comes in a squeezy bottle. Keep adding it until the mixture starts to clump together. When it does, it is ready to roll.

Have the extra coconut ready in a bowl. Take walnut-size mounds of the mixture and drop them into the coconut, roll them around to coat, then shape them into perfect balls.

Store them in an airtight container in the fridge. They can keep for up to a month, not that they last that long very often, but they're great for providing you with a regular sweet treat when you need one.

FLORENTINE COOKIES

Any leftover truffles can be made into Florentine cookies. Preheat the oven to 180°C/fan 160°C and line a baking tray with greaseproof paper. Place however many truffles you have left on the tray, spacing them apart. With the base of a glass, squash each truffle so it is 5–7mm thick and bake for 8 minutes. Cool on a rack.

MAKES: ABOUT 25   TOTAL TIME: 30 MINUTES

Two of the things I always have in the house are chocolate bars and ready-rolled pastry. For emergencies and for life in general. Put the two together and you have a pretty quick dessert – best of all, there is enough to make and put away for a rainy day.

CHOC BAR PUFFS

2 x 320g sheets of
  ready-rolled puff pastry

a little flour, for dusting

8 full-size chocolate bars, the
  kind that lend themselves
  to being melted, halved

1 egg, beaten

cocoa powder, for dusting

Dust your rolling pin with a little flour. Roll out one of the sheets of pastry, leaving it on the backing paper, and pop it on to a baking tray. Have another baking tray ready close by.

Place the bars evenly in line on the pastry, 5 across, 3 up, making sure to leave a good gap between the pieces of chocolate. There will be one extra – you're welcome, that's for you!

Take the second sheet of pastry and roll it out to 1.5cm bigger on each side than the other sheet. (This has to go over the chocolate, so it needs a bit more give.)

Brush all the edges of the first sheet of pastry around the chocolate with most of the egg. Now place the other piece of pastry on top. Using the side of your palm, press down gently around the cubes of chocolate to attach the top to the base. Once it is all sealed, pop it into the fridge for 5 minutes.

Preheat the oven to 200°C/fan 180°C. Take the pastry off the tray and cut out the little chocolate-filled cubes. Brush with the leftover egg. If you want a slightly more grown-up taste, you can sprinkle them with sea salt flakes. Divide them between the two trays and pop them into the oven for 30 minutes, switching the trays around halfway so they get an even bake and even golden-ness.

Once they are out of the oven, dust them with a little cocoa powder. If you are planning to freeze some, don't dust those with cocoa. Let them cool, then freeze in a freezer bag.

These are so easy and quick, because there is no peeling of apples, no coring or chopping, so you can have your pie and eat it too. The filling is a mixture of apple sauce mixed with spices, dried fruit and nuts, then wrapped in filo, perfect enough to fit in the palm of your hand and in your mouth, in a bite, or two. They freeze well, so when you need pie, be it for yourself or for guests, you're always one step ahead.

APPLE PALM PIES

2 x 285g jars of apple sauce, chunky

½ teaspoon mixed spice

50g mixed nuts, or nuts of your choice, roughly chopped

50g raisins

cooking oil spray

270g pack of filo pastry, or 6 sheets

demerara sugar, for sprinkling

Put the apple sauce, mixed spice, nuts and raisins into a bowl, stir well and set aside.

Preheat the oven to 200°C/fan 180°C. Have a 12-hole muffin tray at the ready. Spray the inside of each hole liberally with oil.

Unroll the filo pastry on to a work surface. Stack all 6 sheets on top of each other and, using kitchen scissors, cut out all the pastry in one go to make 8 equal squares, which should give you 48 squares in total. Keep the squares you're not working with under a tea towel to prevent them drying out.

Take 1 square of filo and spray it with oil, lay another square on top, spray again, then lay another on top and spray again. You should have three squares oiled together. It doesn't matter if the squares are a bit off-centre. Place inside the oiled cavity of the muffin tray, press down, and repeat this process until you have filled all 12 holes in the muffin tray.

Fill each hole with an equal amount of the apple filling.

Take another square of filo and spray well, then fold in half and in half again to create a small square. Place the small square on top of the apple mixture and fold the pointy edges inwards. If any areas feel dry, spray with oil. Repeat for all 12, then sprinkle with sugar and bake for 14–16 minutes.

Leave to cool in the tin for 10 minutes. These are best eaten warm, with ice cream or custard.

Any leftover pies can be cooled and frozen. I know 12 wouldn't last very long in my household, so due to the ease of making these, why not double the ingredients and make another full 12 to freeze, providing you have freezer space!

MAKES: 12   ACTIVE TIME: 20 MINUTES   TOTAL TIME: 45 MINUTES

Shrikand is a traditional Gujarati dessert made with a base of strained yoghurt that's flavoured, so sometimes when I want a lighter dessert this is great – and I have a way of making two desserts into one with this. Yoghurt has the ability to take on flavour, so you could go wild and do all sorts. I love the aroma of traditional flavours and scents. With this recipe you'll make a batch of ice cream for later too – but if you'd prefer to just make the dessert for today, simply halve all ingredients.

SAFFRON ROSE SHRIKAND

For the shrikand

1kg Greek yoghurt

1 tablespoon whole milk

10 strands of saffron

600ml double cream

6 tablespoons icing sugar

1 teaspoon cornflour

5 drops of rose
extract/essence

To serve

Shortbread or brandy snaps

pistachios and rose petals

Start by straining the yoghurt through some strong kitchen paper. Line a sieve with the paper, then spoon in all the yoghurt and set aside over a bowl.

Heat the milk in the microwave, then add the strands of saffron and allow the colour to bleed. The warmer the milk the stronger the colour, so get it as warm as you can, which should only take a few seconds.

Put the cream into a bowl with the icing sugar and cornflour and whisk until you have soft peaks. This is not traditional, but I like to add the cream to make it a tiny bit richer, and the cornflour helps to stabilize the cream. Be sure not to clear away the beaters, as you will need them again in a few minutes.

Add the strained yoghurt to the whipped cream and fold through with the saffron-infused milk. Once it is all one even golden colour, stir in the rose extract.

Serve in small dishes with shortbread, or in brandy snaps, which is my personal favourite, and sprinkle over the pistachios and rose petals. Do the same with the ice cream when you serve it.

SHRIKAND ICE CREAM

If you made the full batch, take half of the mixture and put it into another bowl, with 4 tablespoons of golden syrup. This is an excuse to make shrikand ice cream: simply whisk the golden syrup in and transfer to a freezer-safe Tupperware container. Pop the ice cream tub inside a ziplock bag and put it into the freezer. Shrikand for now, ice cream for later.

This is one of those cakes that looks suspiciously boring, plain even, but the three citrus fruits really pack it with a zing. It's simple and easy to make, and as it bakes it creates a delicious curd-like sauce that sits at the bottom, so there's no slicing – it's spoons in and serve. I like it with a little pouring cream, because there is always room for more sauce.

SAUCY CITRUS PUDDING

cooking oil spray

3 eggs, yolks and whites separated

50g butter, melted

200g caster sugar

1 lemon, 1 lime, 1 small orange: zest of all 3, plus enough juice from all 3 to make up 100ml (if you don't have enough, just use lemon or lime juice out of a bottle to top it up)

50g plain flour

250ml whole milk

icing sugar, for dusting

pouring cream, to serve (optional)

Preheat the oven to 160°C/fan 140°C and lightly spray the inside of a medium casserole dish with oil.

Put the egg whites into a bowl big enough to whisk them in. Put the butter, sugar, zest and juice, egg yolks, flour and milk into a second bowl.

Using a hand-held mixer, whisk the egg whites until they are firm, meaning that the peaks will hold but the tips will fold back on themselves.

Take the same mixer and whisk the ingredients in the other bowl until you have a smooth, shiny cake batter.

Now add the whisked whites to the batter and fold it through until there are no foamy white bits left. Pour into the dish and bake for 45 minutes. Before serving, you can dust the top with icing sugar if you like. Eat while it's still piping hot.

SERVES: 6   ACTIVE TIME: 15 MINUTES   TOTAL TIME: 1 HOUR

When you see a swirl in a dessert it looks like so much effort has been made, when in reality it's actually quite easy, especially in this case because the sponge itself takes less time to bake than I do to get into bed. It's such a simple recipe – chocolate cake, creamy chocolate filling, all with a hint of lime. Chocolate limes used to be my fave sweets and I still can't resist them when I see them. You can use any jam you have left over at home, but I like lime marmalade – just for recipes like this, though, I'm not such a fan of it on my toast. I've given quantities for the ganache that will give you some extra chocolatey treats, but just halve the ingredients in green if you only want to make the roulade today.

CHOC LIME ROULADE

For the sponge

3 eggs

100g caster sugar, plus extra for dusting

75g plain flour

25g cocoa powder

For the ganache filling

300g dark chocolate, chips or roughly chopped

100ml boiling water

300g cream cheese

4 tablespoons lime marmalade

1 lime, zest only (save the rest of them)

Preheat the oven to 160°C/fan 140°C, and grease and line a medium baking tray with sides or a Swiss roll tin 35cm x 23cm.

Put the eggs and sugar into a bowl and whisk until the mixture has tripled in size and, when the beaters are lifted, leaves ribbons of batter on the surface. This will take up to 5 minutes.

Sift in the flour and cocoa and use a metal spoon to gently bring the mixture together. Keep mixing gently until there is no flour left in the bottom of the bowl.

Pour the mixture into the tin and gently tilt it to encourage the mixture to get into the corners. When it has run as much as possible, carefully, without squashing the air bubbles out of the mixture, use a small spatula to guide the rest so that it covers the tin evenly.

Bake for 8–10 minutes.

Meanwhile take a large sheet of baking paper the same size as the sponge and sprinkle it generously with sugar. As soon as the sponge is baked, tip it upside down straight on to the waiting sugared paper and peel off the lining paper that it was baked on.

Now, with the long edge closest to you, roll up the whole thing, making sure to wrap it with the sugared paper encased in the roll. Leave to cool in the paper on a cooling rack.

continued over page ➡

To make the ganache, put the chocolate into a bowl and microwave in bursts of 10 seconds until you have just a few unmelted pieces of chocolate. Now stir the chocolate – the heat of the bowl will help melt it until smooth. Pour the boiling water a little bit at a time into the chocolate. Don't be alarmed – at first the chocolate will thicken as you stir. Just add a little more water and stir again. Repeat until you have a loose and glossy ganache.

Divide the ganache mixture in half. Put one half aside and add the cream cheese to the other half, whisking well until you have a creamy mixture.

Once the cake has almost cooled, unroll it and remove the baking paper. Spread it with a thin layer of lime marmalade, then sprinkle over the zest. (Keep the limes, hollow them out and fill the cavity with baking powder. If you leave it in the back of your fridge, they will keep everything smelling fresh.)

Now spread a thin layer of the chocolate cream over the sponge. Then, as you did before, roll the sponge as it was until you get to the end. Make sure to have the roll seam-side down.

Drizzle with some of the remaining ganache, if you like, or see below for suggestions on how to use it.

TRUFFLES

Put the leftover ganache into the fridge for at least an hour, until it's firm. When set, take teaspoons of the stuff, roll them into balls, then roll them in cocoa powder. Leave them in the fridge so you can get a chocolatey treat every time you open the fridge door.

The ganache can be saved and turned into delicious truffles. These chocolatey treats are great to make with children on rainy days, and freeze brilliantly.

These are like doughnut, meets cake, meets fritter, meets pakora. They are as fun to eat as they are to make. Crisp and sweet, and easy to demolish the lot. Apart from eating them, there is so much fun in squeezing the batter into the oil and being quick enough to create something that resembles a holey doughnut. To save yourself time you could make the batter the night before and just do the frying when it's time to eat.

STRAWBERRY MILKSHAKE FUNNEL CAKE

oil, for frying

300g self-raising flour

2 tablespoons icing sugar

2 teaspoons baking powder

275ml whole milk

2 eggs

100g strawberry milkshake powder

Start by heating some oil gently in a small pan, just big enough to fry one cake at a time. The oil should come halfway up the sides. I do these in a small pan so that I don't use up too much oil every time I fry.

Put the flour, icing sugar, baking powder, milk and eggs into a bowl and whisk until you have a smooth batter.

Now there are a few ways of making these: you can place all the mixture in a ziplock bag and snip about 5mm off the end. Or you can use a squeezy bottle, although you don't want to squirt anything quickly into oil. I prefer to use a ziplock bag, and when I need to put it down I just use a bag clip to stop the flow.

In one smooth motion, squeeze out the mixture in rounds, making sure that the batter connects to itself so it has something to hold on to. It should look like a spindly doughnut. Fry for roughly 1 minute on each side, or until golden brown. Have a tray lined with kitchen paper at the ready, to drain the funnel cakes. As soon as they come out of the hot oil, sprinkle them generously with the strawberry milkshake powder and get frying the next one.

HANDY TIP

These freeze really well, so if you have any left over, pop them into a freezer bag.

MAKES: ABOUT 20   ·   TOTAL TIME: 30 MINUTES

These are like chocolate fondants, the ones everyone says are notoriously difficult to make. They have a gingerbread biscuit outer casing with a melty ganache in the centre. They're fun to make and even more fun to eat. This recipe will give you 6 fondants to bake now, and another 6 to keep in the freezer for another time.

GINGERBREAD MELT-IN-THE-MIDDLES

For the biscuits

450g plain flour

1 teaspoon bicarbonate
  of soda

3 tablespoons ground ginger

125g butter

175g soft brown sugar

4 tablespoons golden syrup

1 medium egg, beaten

For the filling

200g dark chocolate
  (or milk chocolate if you
  don't like dark, or white
  chocolate if you prefer
  it sweeter), chopped

200ml boiling water

a pinch of salt

1 round of stem ginger,
  grated

Mix together the flour, bicarbonate of soda and ground ginger in a bowl.

In a small pan melt the butter and sugar with the golden syrup. As soon as the sugar has melted, take off the heat and allow to cool for 5 minutes. Stir the beaten egg into the butter mixture and then add to the dry mix.

Bring the mix together until you have a smooth dough. Take away one third of the dough, wrap it in clingfilm, and chill in the fridge. Form the bigger piece of dough into a sausage shape, then divide it into 12 equal balls.

Lightly grease the inside of a 12-hole cupcake tray. Drop a ball of dough into each cavity and mould the dough so it is level on the base and sides and comes right to the top. Place in the fridge to chill.

To make the ganache, put the chopped chocolate into a bowl, pour in the boiling water and stir until you have a smooth mixture. Sprinkle in the salt and the grated stem ginger, and leave to cool. As soon as it is cool, add some to each biscuit cavity, leaving a 1cm gap at the top.

Place in the fridge to chill. Meanwhile, take out the remaining piece of dough and unwrap it. Roll it out, then cut out circles big enough to cover the top of the fondants. Pop a circle on each one, and be sure to pinch the edges to seal in that centre. Freeze for 1 hour.

Preheat the oven to 180°C/fan 160°C. Take the fondants out of the freezer, then pop 6 of them into a bag and return them to the freezer for later. Bake the remaining 6 for 25–27 minutes. Serve hot.

Bake the rest of the fondants from frozen at 180°C/fan 160°C for 30–35 minutes. Be sure to bake them in the same muffin tin, as this will help to retain their shape.

I have this guy who knows everything there is to know about London – born and bred there, he could give Danny Dyer a run for his money, but for the most part I haven't a clue what he says. Between words I understand and the cockney rhyming slang, I tend to nod, unsure, and he laughs at me. This isn't really a cheesecake, but it tastes pretty good – more like lamington meets pasty. Once you feast your mince pies on these, you won't stop stuffing them into your north and south.

LONDON CHEESECAKE

2 sheets of ready-rolled puff pastry

6 tablespoons strawberry jam, no lumps

1 egg yolk, lightly beaten

250g icing sugar

a few teaspoons of whole milk

50g shredded or desiccated coconut

Preheat the oven to 200°C/fan 180°C. Line a baking tray with baking paper.

Unroll the two sheets of pastry and cut each one into 6 equal squares. Pop 6 of the squares on to the tray. Add a tablespoon of jam to the centre of each one, avoiding the edges.

Brush lightly around the edge of each square with the egg yolk, then place another square of pastry on top and gently press the edges. No crimping required. Every one of these that I have bought and eaten has tall sides and no crimping.

Pop them into the fridge for 10 minutes, then bake for 20–25 minutes, until the pastry is golden and puffy.

Leave to cool on a baking rack. As soon as they are totally cool, mix the icing sugar with a teaspoon of milk at a time, until you have a thick icing. Spread the icing all over the top and sprinkle over the coconut immediately, while the icing is still wet.

These look bigger than your belly can eat, but they are light enough to finish. However, if you do have any left over that you haven't iced, you can freeze them.

Tiramisu is coffee, this is not! I don't know what else is left to say. So many will disagree, but go on, give it a little go. This is a great dessert to make ahead, and it will happily rest in the fridge overnight until you're ready to serve it.

GRAPEFRUIT TIRAMISU

3 medium eggs, yolks and whites separated

50g caster sugar

250g mascarpone

1 teaspoon vanilla bean paste

2 grapefruits, zest and 150ml of juice

25–30 sponge fingers

1 tablespoon cocoa powder, for dusting

Have a 1 litre dish at the ready.

Put the egg yolks and sugar into a bowl and whisk until light and mousse-like. It should be pale and fluffy.

Put the mascarpone and vanilla into another bowl and beat until it's just a bit smoother. Add the egg yolk mixture and whisk until smooth.

Whisk the egg whites to stiff peaks. Then add them to the bowl a little at a time, folding gently with each addition.

Mix the grapefruit juice and zest in a bowl. Using 12 of the sponge fingers, dip each one quickly into the juice and arrange in the base of your dish. Pour half of the mascarpone over the top.

Do the same with the next 12 sponge fingers, layering them over the mascarpone. You may need to use a few more, depending on the size of your dish. If there is any extra juice and zest, pour it on top of the sponge fingers. Top with the rest of the mascarpone and level off.

Dust over the cocoa and leave in the fridge for at least 4 hours before serving, but ideally overnight.

SERVES: 6   ACTIVE TIME: 40 MINUTES   TOTAL TIME: 4 HOURS 30 MINUTES

I never really ate rice as a child, apart from boiled white rice, with curry, or pilau with curry. It was our thing, our staple, as people call it. So eating rice any other way never came to mind. But it turns out I can eat rice any which way, for which I am very grateful. Risotto, delicious – but sweet risotto, double delicious. If my rice farmer granddad was still alive, he would be proud. This recipe gives you a dessert today, with some leftover baked arancini balls for another day. If you'd rather not make those this time, simply halve all ingredients.

SWEET RISOTTO

1.5 litres whole milk

600ml double cream

1 tablespoon vanilla bean paste, or a whole vanilla bean, split

100g unsalted butter

1 bay leaf

1 stick of cinnamon

600g risotto rice

1 teaspoon salt

150g caster sugar

pulp from 8 passion fruit

Put the milk and cream into a pan, just bring to the boil, then reduce the heat and leave on a very low heat. If you are using a vanilla pod, pop it into the milk and cream while they are warming.

Heat the butter in a separate large non-stick pan, and as soon as it has melted, add the bay leaf and cinnamon stick and let them sizzle for a minute. Add all the rice and give it a good stir on a medium heat, making sure to move it around all the time. This should take about 5 minutes – you will see the rice starting to change in appearance, the grains looking whiter.

Have a ladle ready and start adding 1 ladleful of the milk mixture at a time. As soon as some of it has evaporated, add some more, and keep doing this until there is no milk left. This can take a good 20–30 minutes.

Once the milk is finished and you have a thick risotto, take off the heat and stir in the salt, sugar and vanilla bean paste, if using. Take out the bay leaf and cinnamon stick.

Put half the mixture into a dish and leave to cool. Eat the other half with the passion fruit pulp drizzled on top.

Refrigerate the cooled rice overnight. The next day, you can make it into sweet arancini balls. See opposite for how to make these.

SWEET ARANCINI BALLS

Crack 2 eggs into a bowl and lightly whisk. Put 70g of breadcrumbs on a plate. Take tablespoons of the cold rice mix and make golf ball-size balls, using wet hands. If you happen to have an ice cream scoop, this is a good way to measure equal amounts of rice.

Dip the balls into the egg, then roll in the breadcrumbs and pop them on to a tray. Put them back into the fridge while you heat about 500ml of vegetable oil in a pan small enough so you can cook just 2 arancini at a time. The oil should come just halfway up the pan. You'll know when the oil is hot enough if you drop in a bit of bread and it sizzles and floats. Carefully drop a rice ball in and fry until the outside is golden. Drain on kitchen paper and serve hot. You can warm some jam and use that as a dipping sauce, or sprinkle them with cinnamon sugar. If you have any sweet arancini balls left over, they can be frozen.

The best kind of cookies are the ones that are homemade, but when I'm short of time, just divvying them up puts me off. So, I have found a way of making my cookie – cookie being the operative word – and eating it too. It's all made in one pan and cooked slowly on the hob till you have a lovely crust but a gooey centre. I always think if you're going to make a cookie mixture, you might as well double it up and have some ready to bake in the freezer. Simply double all the ingredients if you want to do this.

CHOC CHIP PAN COOKIE

150g unsalted butter

160g brown sugar

1 medium egg

½ teaspoon vanilla extract

½ teaspoon almond extract

225g plain flour

½ teaspoon bicarbonate
  of soda

½ teaspoon salt

200g chocolate chips/
  mini multicoloured
  sugar-coated chocolates

Place a small non-stick, thick-based heavy frying pan, about 23cm, on a medium to low heat. Add the butter and allow it to melt, then add the sugar and stir until it has dissolved. Take off the heat and let it cool for a few minutes.

While it's cooling, lightly beat the egg and add the vanilla and almond extracts.

Now add the flour, bicarb and salt to the mixture in the frying pan, followed by the egg mix. Stir until you have a smooth cookie batter.

Press the batter down and sprinkle over the chocolate chips. Now leave on a low heat for 15–20 minutes. If you find the bottom catches, you may find it helpful to pop a lid on the pan for 5 minutes. What you should end up with is a crisp base and gooey top.

Let it cool and set for about 15 minutes before you start eating. I like to take out slices and eat them hot with ice cream.

HANDY TIP

If you have made a double batch of batter, halve it before cooking, then roll this batch into walnut-sized balls, place on a baking tray lined with greaseproof paper and pop in the freezer. Once frozen, transfer to a labelled freezer bag.

When you want to bake, preheat the oven to 160°C/fan 140°C, pop the frozen cookies on a lined baking tray and bake for 20–25 minutes. Leave on the tray for 10 minutes before eating.

SERVES: 6   ACTIVE TIME: 10 MINUTES   TOTAL TIME: 45 MINUTES

These are like scones, but not; they are like Welsh cakes, but not those either. They are a weird hybrid of the two that I like to fill with pecans and top with salted caramel and coffee cream. I always make enough to reserve half of these rounds, so I can pop them into freezer bags for another occasion.

PECAN ROUNDS WITH COFFEE CREAM

For the rounds

450g plain flour

170g caster sugar

½ teaspoon salt

1 teaspoon baking powder

100g butter

100g pecans, finely chopped

2 eggs, beaten

100g melted butter,
  for brushing

For the coffee cream

2 tablespoons instant coffee

1 tablespoon hot water

300ml double cream

2 tablespoons caster sugar

To serve

salted caramel

Start by making the pecan rounds. Preheat the oven to 180°C/fan 160°C. Grease two baking trays and line with baking paper.

Put the flour, sugar, salt, baking powder and butter into a bowl, and rub the butter in until you have breadcrumbs. Stir in the pecans.

Make a well in the centre and add the eggs, then use a palette knife to bring the dough together. Roll it out on a floured surface to a thickness of 1cm, and cut out rounds using a 6cm cutter. Collect the scraps and keep re-rolling and cutting until you have used up all the dough.

Brush the baking paper in the trays with melted butter. Place the rounds on the trays with small gaps between them and brush again with butter. Bake for 20 minutes, then take them out and leave them to cool on a rack.

Add the coffee to the hot water and leave it to cool completely. Whisk the cream and sugar to soft peaks, then add the cold coffee mixture and whisk it through quickly.

To serve, slather some salted caramel over the rounds and spoon on some of the coffee cream.

Whatever does not get eaten can be frozen.

MAKES: 32   ACTIVE TIME: 40 MINUTES   TOTAL TIME: 1 HOUR

This traybake combines salty, sweet and zesty flavours. It's an assault on the senses but in a good way. Something a little different, but not steering too far away from the classics. While you're making up the batter, you might like to make an extra cake for the freezer – so just double up the cake ingredients if so.

PRESERVED LEMON TRAYBAKE

For the cake

225g unsalted butter

225g caster sugar

275g self-raising flour, sifted

1 teaspoon baking powder

4 large eggs

4 tablespoons whole milk

1 lemon, zest only

For the topping

2 preserved lemons

1 x 170g tin of evaporated milk

Preheat the oven to 160°C/fan 140°C. Grease and line a 30cm x 23cm traybake tin.

Put the butter, sugar, flour, baking powder, eggs, milk and zest into a mixing bowl and mix on a high speed for 2 minutes, until you have a smooth, shiny batter. Pour it into the prepared tin and level the top.

Bake in the oven for 35–40 minutes.

Discard any pips from the preserved lemons, then blitz with the evaporated milk and pass through a sieve.

While the cake is still hot, spread the salty lemony milk all over it, so it can be absorbed. After 15 minutes, remove the cake from the tin and it is ready to slice. This can be eaten cold, but is best warm.

The cake freezes well – just wrap it in foil and then tightly in clingfilm.

MAKES: 12 SQUARES   ACTIVE TIME: 20 MINUTES   TOTAL TIME: 1 HOUR

These are like regular éclairs, but there isn't anything regular about them. Once they're filled with raspberry ripple cream, you stick a stick in, freeze them and then cover them in chocolate – ice lolly, meets dessert, meets pastry. A guaranteed amazing dessert ready to go in your freezer.

RIPPLE ÉCLAIR POPS

For the choux

125ml milk

125ml water

125g butter

150g plain flour, sieved

a pinch of salt

2 teaspoons sugar

4 medium eggs, beaten

For the filling

600ml double cream

3 tablespoons golden syrup

1 teaspoon vanilla extract

150g raspberries, blended
    and sieved

2 tablespoons icing sugar

To finish

18 lolly sticks

600g dark chocolate, melted

100g roasted hazelnuts,
    chopped (optional)

Start by making the choux. Preheat the oven to 200°C/fan 180°C and line two baking rays with baking paper, lightly greased.

Put the milk and water into a pan with the butter and bring to the boil. Take it off the heat, then add the flour, salt and sugar in one go and beat vigorously until you have a smooth paste. Pop it back on the heat to cook the flour out for 2 minutes.

Take the pan off the heat again and empty the dough into a bowl. Now add the eggs a little at a time. Keep mixing after each addition and it will come together. When all the eggs are used up, you should have a smooth, glossy paste. Pop it into a piping bag and snip off the corner to make a 1.5cm hole.

Slowly pipe 10cm lines of dough a couple of centimetres wide on to the baking trays, leaving a 2.5cm gap in between. Once you have done them all, reduce the oven temperature to 180°C/fan 160°C and bake them for 25 minutes.

Take them out of the oven and pierce a hole in the base of each with the back of a wooden spoon, then put them back into the oven, hole side up, to dry out. Take out after 5 minutes and leave to cool completely while you make the cream.

Whip the cream, golden syrup and vanilla to soft peaks. Mix the sieved raspberries with the icing sugar and ripple through the cream. Pop the cream into a piping bag and start to fill each éclair through the little hole, until the piping bag gets pushed out. You may have to twist the tip about to try and get as much cream into it as possible.

Lay the eclairs on a tray quite close together and top with a layer of baking paper. Pop a stick into the rounded end of each one and freeze. They will need at least an hour. Just before taking them out of the freezer, melt the chocolate. There are two ways of eating these. Dip and eat while the chocolate slowly sets. Or dip, then sprinkle the nuts over and freeze for another hour.

If we can use ginger as a spice in cake, somewhere in my mind black pepper feels acceptable too. It's a subtly scented spice that works so well in a sticky cake like this. Try it, if only out of curiosity. This is another sponge that you can make ahead and keep in the freezer or make a couple so you have one now and one for later (double all ingredients if you'd like to do this).

BLACK PEPPER CAKE

75g plain flour

2 heaped teaspoons ground
   black pepper

½ teaspoon bicarbonate
   of soda

2 tablespoons whole milk

150g treacle

75g butter

75g light brown sugar

75ml water

1 large egg, beaten

Preheat the oven to 170°C/fan 150°C and line a 900g loaf tin.

Sift the flour and pepper into a large bowl. Mix the bicarbonate of soda and milk in a separate small bowl and set aside.

Heat the treacle, butter, sugar and water in a pan until dissolved. Let it cool a bit, then add to the dry mix and mix to a smooth, shiny batter. Add the egg and mix in well, then stir in the milk and bicarb mixture.

Spoon into the loaf tin and bake for 1 hour, or until a skewer comes out clean.

Malai ice cream is a subtly scented milk-based ice cream that you can find in South East Asia and often here too. This is my no-churn version – it goes really well with the sweet tatin, but will also go further, leaving enough for a few extra desserts.

BANANA TARTE TATIN WITH MALAI ICE CREAM

For the ice cream

1 x 397g tin of condensed milk

500ml double cream

5 cardamom pods, seeds removed and crushed

For the banana tarte tatin

1 x 500g block of puff pastry

100g brown sugar

75g butter

30–50g chopped hazelnuts

4 or maybe 5 bananas, sliced into 2cm coins

Make the ice cream first. Put the condensed milk, cream and crushed cardamom seeds into a bowl. Whip until thick and at soft peak stage, then transfer to a freezer-safe tub and level the top. Place inside a ziplock bag and freeze.

Now on to the tarte tatin. Preheat the oven to 180°C/fan 160°C and have a 23cm oven-safe pan at the ready.

Roll out the pastry to a 1cm thickness, then cut out a circle about 2cm wider than your pan. Pop it on a baking tray and leave it in the fridge while you make the caramel.

Put the sugar and butter into the pan, and when the sugar dissolves, turn up the heat and allow the caramel to get dark and thicken. Lift the pan and give it all a little swirl occasionally. The main thing is to watch it until it is a deep caramel colour, because once it gets to that point it can burn quickly. Take off the heat and sprinkle on the hazelnuts.

Add the bananas to the caramel, then lay the pastry on top and gently lift and tuck it around the sides of the pan, being careful of the hot caramel. Cut a slit in the top for the steam to escape, and bake for 25–30 minutes.

Let it stand for at least 20 minutes after it comes out of the oven. Then turn it over on to a serving plate and serve with the ice cream.

From the moment I first made these cinnamon goodies I have been addicted. They are delicious, and there is nothing better than incorporating warm cinnamon flavours into a cake. These can be cut into squares and frozen, so you don't have to eat them all at once unless you really want to.

CARAMELIZED BISCUIT TRAYBAKE

For the cake

250g unsalted butter

250g soft dark brown sugar

100g caramelized biscuit smooth spread

½ teaspoon ground cinnamon

½ teaspoon salt

5 medium eggs

300g plain flour, sifted

For the topping

200g white chocolate

200ml double cream

150g crunchy caramelized biscuits, crushed

Preheat the oven to 170°C/fan 150°C. Grease and line a 33cm x 24cm rectangular brownie tray.

Put the butter and sugar into a mixing bowl and whisk until the mixture is light and pale and fluffy. Add the biscuit spread, cinnamon and salt, and mix well.

Add the eggs one at a time, stirring each one in, then fold in the flour until you have an even, smooth, shiny batter. Spread it in the brownie tray and level the top.

Bake for 25-30 minutes, then take out and leave to cool completely in the tray.

Meanwhile make the topping. Put the white chocolate into a bowl. Heat the cream in a pan until it just comes to the boil, then take off the heat and pour over the chocolate. Let it sit for half a minute . . . don't be tempted to stir just yet. When the chocolate starts to melt, stir until the mixture is silky smooth.

Stir in the crushed biscuits, then spread all over the cooled cake. Once the topping has set, lift the cake out of the tray, using the paper to help you, and cut it into squares.

MAKES: 18 SQUARES   ACTIVE TIME: 40 MINUTES   TOTAL TIME: 2 HOURS

I had always imagined that baklava would be very sweet, like Indian sweets, and I wasn't wrong – it is sweet, but there's something about the crunchy, sticky pastry and nuts that makes you forget. This is my favourite combination of chocolate and orange, and I like to eat it the way we did in Turkey, with lashings of clotted cream on top.

CHOCOLATE AND ORANGE BLOSSOM BAKLAVA

300g mixed nuts

3 tablespoons golden syrup

½ teaspoon salt

2 tablespoons cocoa powder

1 orange, zest only (save the juice for the syrup)

200g butter

2 x 270g packs of filo pastry

2 x 140g pots of clotted cream

For the syrup

250g caster sugar

50g honey

3 teaspoons orange blossom water

orange juice, freshly squeezed and topped with water to make 200ml of liquid

4 cardamom pods, crushed

Preheat the oven to 160°C/fan 140°C. Grease a square 21cm cake tin.

In a food processor, blitz the nuts until ground to small, even pieces. Stir in the syrup, salt, cocoa powder and orange zest and put to one side.

Melt the butter, then open your first pack of filo pastry. Cut the sheets in half so you have a pile of squares. Place your cake tin on top and trim the pastry with a sharp knife so it is the same size as the base of the tin.

Brush a square of pastry with butter and lay it in the base of the cake tin, then do the same to every single square until you have all that pastry inside the tin. Press the pastry down firmly every time you put in a square. Put the nuts on top and press down again to create an even layer.

Open the second pack of pastry and, again, cut it in half and trim the edges to fit the tin. Layer each piece one on top of the other as before, brushing with melted butter, and pressing down. If there's any butter left over, just pour it on top.

With the pastry still in the tin, use a sharp knife to cut out the squares, making sure to get all the way to the bottom layer. Bake for 20 minutes, then reduce the heat to 130°C/fan 110°C and bake for a further 45 minutes.

To make the syrup, mix together the sugar, honey, orange blossom water and juice. Add the crushed cardamom pods and let them infuse for a couple of minutes, then remove. Bring to the boil, then reduce to a simmer for 10 minutes. Once the baklava is out of the oven, pour the syrup all over and leave to cool completely.

I like to decorate these with edible golden stars. They are best eaten with a smothering of clotted cream.

MAKES: 16   ACTIVE TIME: 40 MINUTES   TOTAL TIME: 2 HOURS

Sometimes when I want a quick dessert I want to make some elements of it and buy the others – that makes me feel less like I've done nothing and better because I've done a little something, no matter how insignificant. I love hot and cold and texture, so this is my recipe for hot burnt butterscotch over room-temp rice pudding out of a tin, with freezing cold ice cream. There is enough sauce here to either freeze for another time, or make frappés (see below).

BURNT BUTTERSCOTCH BANANAS
WITH ICE CREAM AND RICE PUDDING

300g unsalted butter

500g light brown sugar

600ml double cream

a pinch of salt

3 bananas, sliced

2 x 400g tins of rice pudding

vanilla ice cream

Put the butter into a medium non-stick pan and melt over a medium heat. Keep the butter on the heat until it is foamy and golden brown – about 4–5 minutes.

Stir in the sugar and the cream, then reduce the heat and cook gently for 7–10 minutes, stirring continuously until the mixture thickens. Add the salt.

Take off the heat and let it cool for a bit. Don't forget this is boiling sugar, so be careful. Place half in a freezer-safe Tupperware container and set aside. Add the sliced bananas to the rest of the sauce and mix through.

To serve, divide the rice pudding between your bowls, then pour on the burnt banana butterscotch and add a dollop of ice cream.

BURNT BUTTERSCOTCH FRAPPÉ

For the leftover butterscotch, frappé is all I'm saying. To make 2 drinks take 2 large handfuls of ice cubes, 4 tablespoons butterscotch sauce, 100ml strong black coffee and 300ml whole milk.

Blend the lot in a blender and pour into glasses. Add some whipped cream straight out of a can and drizzle with a little more butterscotch sauce.

SERVES: 4   TOTAL TIME: 30 MINUTES

So this is an actual thing, and I saw it when I was scrolling through social media. That last bit of milk at the bottom of the cereal bowl is the best bit – it has all the sugar and all the flavour – so it feels only right to turn it into an ice cream.

CEREAL MILK ICE CREAM

1.2 litres double cream

150g Frosties cereal, plus extra for sprinkling

200ml condensed milk

5 tablespoons golden syrup

Pour the cream into a large bowl, and add the cereal, condensed milk and golden syrup. Stir well, making sure the cereal is submerged, then leave to sit for an hour or more in the fridge, to make sure the cream is cold enough to whip.

Drain the cereal out of the milk and pop it into another bowl. Don't forget to have a bowl underneath the sieve, or you'll lose that precious cream.

Whip the cream mixture to soft peaks.

Using the back of a fork, mash up the cereal just a little bit. Fold it into the cream mixture, using the fork to help separate the flakes of soggy cereal.

Pour into a freezer-safe, airtight container and sprinkle over some extra cereal to cover the top completely. Put the lid on, then pop into a large ziplock bag – this will ensure that you always have a soft scoop as it will prevent the ice cream from hardening – and freeze for a minimum of 2 hours.

This biscuit base is beautiful, with its dark black cocoa colour contrasting with the pink pannacotta. Whenever I have pannacotta I feel like it needs something crunchy to go with it, and this is exactly that in a tart. Another great dessert for making ahead, as you can just pop it in the fridge until you're ready to serve it chilled.

CHOCOLATE ROSE PANNACOTTA TART

For the tart shell

24 black and white sandwich
    cookies

85g butter, melted

For the ganache layer

100g milk chocolate

100ml boiling water

For the rose pannacotta

3½ leaves of gelatine

200ml whole milk

300ml double cream

25g caster sugar

1 teaspoon rose extract

a few drops of pink gel
    food colouring

Have a 25cm fluted loose-bottomed round tart tin ready. Put the cookies into a food processor and blitz to fine crumbs. Mix in the butter, then transfer to the tart shell and spread all over the base and sides. Pop into the freezer for 15 minutes.

To make the ganache, put the chocolate into a bowl and microwave in bursts of 10 seconds, until you have just a few pieces of unmelted chocolate remaining. Now stir the chocolate – the heat from the bowl will help melt it until smooth. Pour the hot water a little at a time into the chocolate. Don't be alarmed. At first the chocolate will thicken as you stir. Add another bit of water and stir. Repeat this, stirring until you have a glossy mixture. Leave to cool.

Now get started on the pannacotta by soaking the gelatine leaves in cold water. Put the milk, cream and sugar into a pan and bring to a simmer, then turn off the heat – the sugar will have melted. Drain the gelatine, squeeze out any excess liquid, then stir into the milk and cream mix. Add the rose extract and pink colouring, and leave to cool for 30 minutes.

In the meantime, pour the ganache into the tart tin and pop back into the freezer to set.

When the pannacotta is only warm to touch, pour it into the tart tin and leave to chill for at least 2 hours before eating.

SERVES: 8   ACTIVE TIME: 30 MINUTES   TOTAL TIME: 3 HOURS

One day I want to go to Sweden and eat one of these, right on its own soil. I have made many of them, but this is a simplified one, using as many elements as possible from the cake without having to make the tricky marzipan dome. Same delicious taste, with a new look.

PRINCESS TORTE CAKE

For the custard

600ml milk

1 teaspoon vanilla
  bean paste

3 egg yolks

125g caster sugar

50g cornflour, plus extra
  for dusting

For the cake

250g caster sugar

8 medium eggs

250g plain flour, sifted

To finish

2 limes, zest only

a few drops of green gel
  food colouring

250g white marzipan

250g raspberry jam

Start by making the custard so it has plenty of time to chill. Heat the milk and vanilla in a pan until it comes up to a simmer, then take the pan off the heat.

Put the egg yolks, sugar and cornflour into a bowl and whisk until the mixture is light and fluffy. This takes about 5 minutes. Slowly add the warm milk, whisking all the time, until all the milk has gone in. Pour the mixture back into the pan and mix slowly over a low to medium heat until the custard becomes really thick. Take off the heat and transfer to a bowl. Give it a few minutes to cool, then cover and chill in the fridge.

Start the sponge now. Preheat the oven to 160°C/fan 140°C, and grease and line two 23cm round cake tins. When you cut out the two rounds of paper for the base, cut out a third to use as a template for the marzipan.

Whisk the sugar and eggs in a mixer for 10 minutes on high speed, until the mixture has tripled in size. Fold the flour in gently with a large metal spoon, being careful not to knock out all that air.

Divide the mixture between the two tins and bake for 25–30 minutes.

While the cakes are baking, add the zest and the green colouring to the marzipan and knead it until you get an even colour. Roll out and make a 23cm circle, using your extra circle of baking paper. Dust the surface with a little bit of cornflour to prevent the marzipan sticking, and pop it into the freezer to firm up a little.

Take the cakes out of the oven and cool on a wire rack. Slice each cake in half horizontally, and sandwich them back together with raspberry jam.

Place one cake on your serving dish. Pop the custard into a piping bag and pipe kisses on top. Brush the top of the next cake with a tiny bit of jam to act as glue and lay the marzipan on top. Then place this cake on top of the custard.

When this cake isn't being eaten, it needs to be kept in the fridge. To serve, add a fresh rose on top.

SERVES: 8   ACTIVE TIME: 1 HOUR   TOTAL TIME: 2 HOURS 30 MINUTES

After my travels in Nepal last year, I became enamoured with food in little parcels. I already love samosas, so it's no wonder I love these little parcels with sweet and savoury fillings. I have made various versions of these, and this is one of my favourites. These are made with a chocolate pastry and filled with chocolate and nuts, with a quick raspberry dip to go with them.

CHOCO MOMO WITH RASPBERRY SAUCE

For the pastry

220g plain flour

30g cocoa powder

2 tablespoons vegetable oil

a pinch of salt

boiling water

For the filling

100g chocolate
  hazelnut spread

100g mixed nuts, finely
  chopped

For the sauce

150g raspberries, fresh
  or frozen

3 tablespoons icing sugar

1 tablespoon lemon juice

Start by making the pastry. Put the flour into a bowl with the cocoa powder and mix well. Mix in the oil and salt, then make a well in the centre and add boiling water a little at a time until the dough starts to come together. It will still be too floury at this point, and that's okay.

As soon as the dough is cool enough to handle, get your hands in and bring it together. If it's still too floury, add a little water, a tablespoon at a time, until all the dough is in one piece and there is no flour left. It should not be wet or tacky. Knead the dough for a few minutes on a work surface until it is smooth and shiny.

To make the filling, mix the chocolate hazelnut spread and nuts together and set aside. You can also make the sauce now, by blitzing the raspberries, icing sugar and lemon juice together to make a smooth sauce. I like to make it extra smooth by passing it through a sieve.

To make the momos, roll the dough out into a long sausage about 40cm long on a very lightly floured surface. Cut it into 20 equal pieces, then roll each piece into a disc about 10cm in diameter. While you'll rolling, cover the rest of the dough with a damp tea towel to stop it drying out.

Add a small teaspoon of filling to the centre of each disc. There are various ways of sealing a momo, and there are tutorials online. But for a basic shape, just use your finger to brush a small amount of water around the edges, then simply bring the dough to the centre and pinch to seal it tightly.

To cook these, they need steaming. You can freeze them at this point if you want. I have a steamer that sits on top of a pan of boiling water, but you can use an electric steamer, a bamboo steamer or even a colander placed on top of a pan of boiling water with a lid that fits tightly.

Cut a small piece of greaseproof paper for each momo to sit on. Place the momos inside the steamer in batches and steam for 12–15 minutes. The pastry should puff out and become glossy. Once steamed, they are ready to eat.

Ras malai is Bengali for 'juice creams'. They are these little bits of cake that bob around in gently spiced milk, like a floating cheesecake thing. This is my version without the floating. Same delicious flavours – rich, creamy and lightly spiced and fragrant.

RAS MALAI CAKE

For the cake

10 strands of saffron, dropped into 4 tablespoons of warm milk

250g unsalted butter

250g caster sugar

5 medium eggs, beaten

250g self-raising flour

1 teaspoon baking powder

For the milk drizzle

100g milk powder

150ml boiling water

cardamom seeds, removed from the pods and ground

For the buttercream

2 cardamom pods, crushed

3 tablespoons whole milk

300g unsalted butter, softened

600g icing sugar, sifted

To decorate

edible rose petals, mixed with 100g roughly chopped pistachios

Preheat the oven to 170°C/fan 150°C. Grease and line two 20cm sandwich tins.

Make the saffron milk. Place the butter and sugar in a bowl and whisk until light and fluffy and almost white. Add the eggs a little at a time, making sure to keep whisking. Then add the flour, baking powder and saffron milk, and fold the mixture until you have a smooth, shiny batter.

Divide the mixture between the two tins and level the tops. Bake for 20–25 minutes.

Meanwhile, make the milk drizzle by mixing the milk powder with the boiling water in a bowl. Add the ground cardamom seeds and mix. As soon as the cakes are out of the oven, drizzle some of the milk all over the top of both cakes and leave in the tin for at least 10 minutes before turning them out and removing them to cool on a rack.

To make the buttercream, put the crushed cardamom pods in a small bowl of the milk and leave to infuse.

Meanwhile, put the butter into a mixing bowl and whisk until very soft and light in colour. Add the icing sugar a little at a time, whisking after each addition, until all combined. Then pour the cardamom milk through a sieve into the buttercream and whisk until really light and fluffy.

Once the cakes are totally cool, place one cake on your serving dish and spread an even layer of buttercream over it. Put the other cake on top. Flip the cake over so the milk drizzle top becomes the bottom and sandwiches the buttercream. Spread some buttercream evenly across the top and the sides and use a ruler to level off the edges.

If you have any cream left over you can pipe little kisses on top. Then gently take the rose petals and pistachios and press them into the bottom edge of the cake.

BASICS

DRY SPICE

MAKES: A 110g JAR   **TOTAL TIME:** 5 MINUTES

12 kaffir lime leaves

2 nori sheets

10g ground ginger

20g garlic granules

30g onion granules

20g celery salt

1 teaspoon table salt

10g chilli flakes

10g white sesame seeds

10g black sesame seeds
(if you can't find these,
you can just use the same
amount of white)

2 teaspoons dried coriander

This incredibly versatile, flavourful spice mix is perfect for marinades or to use as a rub on meats and vegetables. I often use this to make my super-quick version of instant noodles – cook 40g noodles per person, and stir a teaspoon of this through it. Add a teaspoon of the spice paste from p. 78 too, if you like.

Grind the lime leaves and nori sheets to a fine powder. Add to a medium sized jar along with all the other ingredients. Put the lid on and shake to mix through to make sure it is all well incorporated.

BENGALI SPICE MIX (*PANCH PHORAN*)

MAKES: A 100g JAR   **TOTAL TIME:** 5 MINUTES

20g nigella seeds

20g mustard seeds

20g fennel seeds

20g cumin seeds

20g fenugreek seeds

You'll find this in my Corned Beef Bombay Pie (p. 118) and Watercress Quinoa Kedgeree (p. 119) but it's a great one to have in your cupboard all the time. It goes brilliantly with meat, fish, vegetables and lentils. All you need is equal amounts of the five spices listed, so if you don't want to make a whole jar, simply reduce the quantities. It works well ground into pastries for added flavour, or simply cook it in some oil at the start of any stew or curry to add something a little bit special.

Grind all the ingredients together until fine, then transfer to a clean dry jar to store.

THAI GREEN CURRY PASTE

MAKES: APPROX. 900g   TOTAL TIME: 25 MINUTES

150ml oil

3 bulbs of garlic, peeled

250g ginger, peeled and
    chopped into chunks

1 medium onion, peeled and
    roughly chopped

90g lemongrass (6 sticks),
    fibrous outer layer removed

3g pack of kaffir lime leaves

3 limes, zest and juice

10 small green finger chillies

25g coriander, stalks and all

75ml fish sauce

1 tablespoon brown sugar

2 tablespoons salt

Yes, you can buy this in a shop, but the flavours are so much more powerful when you make your own.

Place all the ingredients into a blender and whiz till you have a smooth paste. This is enough for two decent sized curries. The paste will differ in consistency depending on how juicy the limes are and how fresh the ginger is.

To make a curry, all it needs is either 400g of cooked king prawns, or 500g of diced chicken breast if you prefer, with some green beans or veg of your choice and a 400ml tin of coconut milk.

It can be kept in the fridge for 6 weeks or in the freezer for 3 months.

TANDOORI SPICE MIX

MAKES: A 100g JAR   TOTAL TIME: 5 MINUTES

28g jar ground ginger

41g jar ground cumin

34g jar ground coriander

46g jar paprika

40g jar cayenne

40g salt

60g jar garlic granules

This recipe will make you a huge batch, but I use this in practically everything! You'll need it for the 'Tandoori' Oven Chicken (see p. 178), but it's a great addition to any marinade or curry. It's also good rubbed into fish or chicken, and will work really well as a seasoning for potato wedges or burger patties.

Place all the ingredients in a large jar and shake really well to combine.

MY FAVOURITE CURRY PASTE

MAKES: APPROX. 900g   TOTAL TIME: 25 MINUTES

200ml vegetable oil, plus
  extra for cooking

200g jar of chopped garlic

190g jar of chopped ginger

3 tablespoons garam masala

650g frozen chopped onions,
  thawed

4 tablespoons chilli powder
  (or paprika, if you prefer a
  milder curry)

2 teaspoons ground turmeric

3 tablespoons salt

4 tablespoons honey

4 tablespoons tomato paste

3 teaspoons tamarind paste
  or sauce

1 lemon, juice only

This is one of my favourite bases for a curry. It packs loads of flavour and is so versatile. It works with meat or fish, or just any leftover veg you might have in the fridge.

Put all the ingredients in a food processor and blitz to a smooth paste. Add 3 tablespoons of oil to the base of a pan and heat. Scrape all the mixture from the food processor into the pan, and stir frequently over a medium heat for 20 minutes. The mixture will turn into a rich, dark paste. Once cooked, transfer to a clean jar and leave to cool completely before storing in the fridge. Will keep in the fridge for 1 month, or in the freezer for 3 months.

PANCAKE BATTER

SERVES: 4   TOTAL TIME: 10 MINUTES

250g plain flour

1 teaspoon baking powder

½ teaspoon table salt

3 tablespoons caster sugar

170ml whole milk

2 medium eggs

2 tablespoons vegetable oil

This is one of the quickest things you can whip up in the morning – it practically takes the same amount of time as pouring a bowl of cereal. And it's always a winner with the kids. Top with fruit and maple syrup – or use in the traybake on p. 24. You can also prepare it in advance – and in fact, batter is often better if it has rested – so make it the night before and after a quick stir in the morning, it will be ready to pour into a hot pan.

Make the batter by adding the flour, baking powder, salt and sugar into a bowl. Whisk the dry ingredients together.

Make a well in the centre and add the milk, along with the eggs and oil. Whisk it all until you have a thick, smooth batter.

Heat a non-stick frying pan over a medium heat. Add a knob of butter and swirl it around. Add a large spoonful of batter (or less depending on what sized pancake you'd like to make). Once a few bubbles start to appear, flip it over and cook for a further minute or two until both sides are golden. Serve hot with toppings of your choice.

GARLIC BREAD

MAKES: 12　　TOTAL TIME: 2 HOURS 30 MINUTES　ACTIVE TIME: 30 MINUTES

450g plain flour

7g fast-action yeast

1 teaspoon sugar

5g salt

50g butter

300ml warm water

2 tablespoons coarse
  semolina

75g butter, melted

5 cloves of garlic, grated

a small handful of parsley

a good pinch of rock salt

What meal isn't improved by garlic bread? It's especially lovely along-side my Mushroom Lasagne (p. 156) or Chorizo Fish Stew (p. 168).

Add the flour, yeast, sugar and salt to a bowl. Add the butter and rub it in. Make a well in the centre and add the water. Bring the dough together and knead until it is smooth and stretchy. This takes 5 minutes in a food processor with a dough hook, and 10 minutes by hand.

Put it back into the bowl, cover and leave to prove for 1 hour or till the dough has doubled in size.

Lightly grease a roasting tray and sprinkle semolina over the base. Take the dough and knock it back in the bowl. Tip out on to a floured surface and divide the mix into golf ball sized pieces.

Add the dough balls to the tray leaving small gaps in between to give the dough room to grow. Cover and leave to prove till doubled in size.

Preheat the oven to 160°C/fan 140°C. Bake in the oven for 30-35 minutes.

Meanwhile, melt the butter and add the garlic, parsley and salt. As soon as the rolls come out of the oven, brush all the butter on top.

Any leftovers can be frozen (you could also freeze the uncooked dough balls and cook from frozen).

PITTA

MAKES: 12

ACTIVE TIME: 30 MINUTES   TOTAL TIME: 1 HOUR 30 MINUTES – 2 HOURS 30 MINUTES (DEPENDING ON PROVING TIME)

250g strong bread flour,
   plus extra for dusting

7g fast-action yeast

1 teaspoon salt

4 tablespoons oil

150ml cold water

Another bread staple in my house. You can always make a meal quicker by buying these, but they're so amazing when they're baked fresh. Use with Harissa Bean Pizza (p. 22), Paneer Pitta (p. 104) and Chicken Shawarma (p. 177).

Place the flour in a large bowl. Add the yeast to one side and salt and oil to the other. Give it all a rough mix with your hands.

Make a well in the centre and add the water. Gradually bring the dough together.

Rub the work surface with a little oil and tip the dough out. Knead the dough for about 10 minutes till it's smooth, shiny and very stretchy.

Leave in a bowl, covered with clingfilm or a tea towel, in a warm place for an hour or until the dough has doubled in size.

Preheat the oven to 250°C, or the highest temperature you can get it.

Place a baking tray in the oven.

Tip the dough onto a very lightly dusted surface. Knock out all the air and divide the mixture into 12 equal-sized balls. Roll out each ball into an oval shape, about 3mm thin.

You will need to cook these in batches. Place as many as you can fit on the tray and bake for 2-3 minutes until they are golden brown and puffed up. Repeat with the leftover dough, leaving the baked ones wrapped in teatowels to keep warm.

WHITE BAPS

MAKES: 8   TOTAL TIME: 2 HOURS

500g strong bread flour, plus
  extra for dusting

7g fast-action yeast

2 teaspoons caster sugar

1 teaspoon salt

300ml warm water

5 tablespoons oil

1 egg, for glazing

1 teaspoon poppy seeds

I find it's great to have a reliable recipe for lovely soft white rolls that you can keep returning to again and again. I use these for my Fish Pie Burgers (p. 114) but you can, of course, use them for absolutely anything – the Corned Beef Subs (p. 108), Falafel (p. 100) or Coronation Tuna (p. 96), alongside a soup (p. 130) and absolutely anything else you can think of …

Put the flour into a bowl with the yeast and sugar on one side and the salt on the other. Give them a quick mix, then make a well in the centre. Pour in the water and oil and bring everything together gently until it forms a dough. Tip it out on to a floured work surface and knead until the mixture is elastic and smooth. It will be sticky, but be sure not to add any flour to the work surface.

Place back in the bowl, cover with clingfilm and leave in a warm place to double in size (approx. 1 hour–1 ½ hours).

Take the dough out of its bowl and put it on a lightly floured work surface. Have a baking tray at the ready, lined with baking paper. Knock the air out of the dough and divide into 8 equal balls. Place them on the tray a few centimetres apart, cover with a piece of greased clingfilm and leave to double in size again.

Preheat the oven to 240°C/fan 220°C. Brush the rolls with the beaten egg and sprinkle with poppy seeds. Place in the oven and bake for 10–15 minutes.

Remove from the oven and wrap in a clean tea towel to help absorb any extra moisture as they cool.

HOME-MADE BUTTER

MAKES: APPROX. 250G BLOCK   TOTAL TIME: 30 MINS

600ml double cream

1 tablespoon sea salt

Put the cream into a mixer, or use a hand-held mixer, and whisk on high for about 5 minutes, scraping the sides of the bowl every now and then, until it gets to the soft-peak stage. After that it will quickly get to stiff peaks and then it will curdle. This is exactly what you want. As soon as it does that, it will change fast – you will be able to hear it. There will be a lot of sloshing, where the water separates from the fat. What you should be left with is crumbly looking butter and liquid in the base of the bowl.

Have ready a colander lined with muslin, or a thin piece of cotton (e.g. a clean tea towel). Tip the butter into the colander and leave it for all that excess liquid to drain off. As the dripping slows down, give it a good squeeze to get rid of as much moisture as possible. Pop into a clean bowl, add the salt and mix through until the crystals are dispersed. Now either store in a jar or mould into a block and wrap in parchment paper. Refrigerate until needed.

You can customize this however you like. Some sweet options I like are brown sugar butter, apple butter (simply add apple sauce), cinnamon butter, vanilla butter and strawberry butter (add freeze-dried strawberries).

PEANUT BUTTER

MAKES: A 100G JAR   TOTAL TIME: 5 MINUTES

500g peanuts

1 teaspoon salt – (optional – omit if you use salted peanuts)

1 tablespoon honey

4–5 tablespoons vegetable oil

You'll need peanut butter for my traybake (see p. 24) and the One-Tray Peanut Chicken (see p. 147), but frankly who doesn't need a jar of peanut butter in their cupboard? And it's so much more satisfying when you've made it yourself. You can of course swap in practically any nut you want – almonds and cashews work well, too.

Add the nuts to a processer with the salt and honey and blitz till the whole thing starts to change texture. Add the oil slowly and watch as it turns to butter in front of your very eyes. As soon as it's smooth and shiny, stop and transfer the mixture to a jar.

GRANOLA

MAKES: APPROX. 17 SERVINGS   ACTIVE TIME: 10 MINUTES   TOTAL TIME: 45 MINUTES

3 tablespoons melted
  coconut oil

140ml maple syrup or
  runny honey

1 teaspoon vanilla bean paste

1 teaspoon almond extract

300g rolled oats

100g sunflower seeds

100g flaked almonds

100g dried cranberries/
  blueberries/raisins – or
  a mix if you prefer

Home-made breakfast, all ready to go in the morning. Serve with yoghurt and fresh berries, or with just a dash of milk. Add some chocolate chunks to it for a real treat. You could also use this in the Pruney Granola Cake (p. 43) or the Breakfast Trifle (p. 47).

Preheat the oven to 150°C/fan 130°C and have a large, lined baking tray at the ready. Put the coconut oil, maple syrup, vanilla and almond extract into a bowl and mix together. Add in the oats, sunflower seeds and almonds and mix really well until everything is coated and looking glossy, then spread the mixture out on to the baking tray. Bake for 15 minutes. Remove from the oven and scatter the dried fruit over the oats, then bake again for 15-20 minutes or until the oats are a light golden colour.

Once ready, remove the tray from the oven and allow the granola to cool completely. Once cooled, you may need to break up some of the larger pieces, but it's nice to keep some small nuggets. Store in an airtight jar - it will last for up to a month.

INDEX

THANKS

Writing recipes is the gift that keeps giving and giving. Just imagine . . . My kitchen, not very big, is functional for family and home, but was never created or designed for the force that is recipe writing. When I am in that world I am engulfed and intoxicated in the most harmless, euphoric way possible. I dart around. It looks aimless but I do know where I'm going (most of the time). Tapping a few keys on my laptop, carefully placed away from any liquids. I make quick notes on my jotting pad. Check the oven. Click the timer, wipe down the surface, clear away the toaster, pour a glass of water and fill the dishwasher a little more.

I imagine up a new recipe and there in the back of my mind tick tick ticking away is, What shall I make for dinner? Shall I cook dinner? Or shall I just pop a dinner out of the freezer? Or, they could just eat the cake that I'm testing. It's always my last resort, but great for gathering 'Who's your favourite parent' points.

But once I am out of my writing, crazy-woman phase, once I have cleared up, once everything is put back into its place, once I have wiped away my greasy fingermarks off the handles of the cupboards and disinfected the kitchen to within an inch of its life, the work continues.

So thank you to all of you who have worked so hard to breathe life into this book.

Thank you to the recipe testers, Emma, Rosie and Katy, for going through each recipe one by one and for recognizing the recipes I may have written up at midnight, that nobody could understand, not even me! We got there in the end.

Thank you Chris Terry for your beautiful photography, your really good camera and your bad dad jokes. The only man alive I have seen eat half a cabbage! Good times!

Rob Allison and Rosie Mackean, thank you for all of your help working through these recipes, helping them to look beautiful. It never feels like work with you two around. Which is good, I think. Or is it?

Emma Lahaye, stylist extraordinaire, is there anything you can't do? Don't answer that, I already know the answer. Thank you, my friend.

Thanks as ever to Anne, for dotting the 'i's and crossing the 't's but also for sliding a plate of fruit next to me without saying a word in the hope that I might stop to eat, and always frantically texting 'Don't forget your colourful scarves.' One of these days I might, just to see you flap.

Special thanks to Dan, who from the get-go has believed in me with so much enthusiasm he makes a puppy look docile. For taking time to talk, email and for just being around. Thank you. Not that it takes much, all I have to say is 'food' and Dan will say, 'Where?'

Thank you to the entire team; Bea, you are totally ace, we powered through and got there in the end, not one lunch break was safe, but we did it. Thank you also to Sarah for her amazing design, Emma for shepherding us through the process, Nick, Sarah K, Emma H, Amy, Gail, Alice and Claire.

To my family: Abdal, Musa, Dawud, Maryam. Time is ours, let's have it!